The EVERYTHING®
German Practice Book

Dear Reader,

Learning a different language is a daunting endeavor, but it is not an impossible one. I got a late start in learning languages. When I was in high school, I was too busy to take a foreign language. Now I can read seventeen different languages! The secret to learning a language is practice.

This book will help you practice German. It is a systematic compilation of class notes and materials that I have used in teaching the German language. As you complete the exercises and listen to the CD, you will find that you retain both the grammar and the vocabulary.

The rules may seem hard at first, but as you continue to work through the exercises, they will become easier and easier. To aid this process, you will not only be translating English into German, but also German into English.

If at all possible, visit a German-speaking country like Germany, Austria, or Switzerland, where you can become part of a culture where the German language is the norm. If that isn't practical, make a reservation at a German restaurant and be sure to order in German. How about *Schlachtplatte* and *Schwarzwälder Kirschtorte*, or Westphalian ham with buttered bread and *Steinhäger*? What about some *Linsensuppe* or *heißer Kartoffelsalat*? Or how about *Gulasch, Sauerbraten, Wienerschnitzel, Brunswick Mettwurst, Torte, Käsekuchen, Kartoffelklöße*, and *Apfelstrudel*? The German language is a powerful, regal, and elegant language to learn. With consistent practice, I know that you will increase your German proficiency. Have fun!

Jeffery Donley, Ph.D.

The EVERYTHING® Series

Editorial

Publishing Director	Gary M. Krebs
Director of Product Development	Paula Munier
Associate Managing Editor	Laura M. Daly
Associate Copy Chief	Brett Palana-Shanahan
Acquisitions Editor	Lisa Laing, Gina Chaimanis
Development Editor	Rachel Engelson
Associate Production Editor	Casey Ebert
Language Editor	Ruth Sondermann

Production

Director of Manufacturing	Susan Beale
Associate Director of Production	Michelle Roy Kelly
Cover Design	Paul Beatrice
	Erick DaCosta
	Matt LeBlanc
Design and Layout	Argosy Publishing
	Brewster Brownville
	Colleen Cunningham
	Sorae Lee
	Jennifer Oliveira
Series Cover Artist	Barry Littmann

Visit the entire Everything® Series at *www.everything.com*

THE
EVERYTHING®
GERMAN PRACTICE BOOK

Practical techniques to improve your speaking and writing skills

Jeffery Donley, Ph. D.

Adams Media
Avon, Massachusetts

For my daughter, Jill, who spent much of her summer vacation
helping me with this project—and who was then inspired to take
German as her college foreign language. I love you.

An Everything® Series Book.
Everything® and everything.com® are registered trademarks of F+W Publications, Inc.

Published by Adams Media, an F+W Publications Company
57 Littlefield Street, Avon, MA 02322 U.S.A.
www.adamsmedia.com

ISBN: 1-59337-618-9
Printed in the United States of America.

J I H G F E D C B A

Library of Congress Cataloging-in-Publication Data
Donley, Jeffery.
The everything German practice book / Jeffery Donley.
        p.   cm. -- (The everything series)
ISBN 1-59337-618-9
1. German language--Textbooks for foreign speakers--English.
2. German language--Grammar. 3. German language--Spoken German. I. Title. II. Series.

PF3112.D664 2006
438.2'421--dc22
                                                2006013596

This publication is designed to provide accurate and authoritative information
with regard to the subject matter covered. It is sold with the understanding that
the publisher is not engaged in rendering legal, accounting, or other professional advice. If legal advice or other expert assistance is required, the services of a
competent professional person should be sought.
        —From a *Declaration of Principles* jointly adopted by a Committee of the
American Bar Association and a Committee of Publishers and Associations

Many of the designations used by manufacturers and sellers to distinguish their
products are claimed as trademarks. Where those designations appear in this
book and Adams Media was aware of a trademark claim, the designations have
been printed with initial capital letters.

This book is available at quantity discounts for bulk purchases.
For information, please call 1-800-872-5627.

Contents

Acknowledgments

Thank you to my editor, Gina Chaimanis, for your professionalism, creativity, hard work, and most of all, your belief in me as a writer. I wish you the best in your new endeavors.

I'd also like to thank Kate Powers for her help in the completion of the project. Thank you for your professionalism and kindness.

Top Ten Reasons to Practice Your German

1. You'll be more likely to pass a German proficiency test required for a degree of higher learning.

2. You'll be able to order your meal in a German restaurant.

3. You'll be able to read German literature in the author's native language.

4. You'll increase your value to your present and/or future employers.

5. You'll be able to interact with the local citizens when you travel to Germany, Austria, and Switzerland.

6. You'll have the confidence and pride that comes from mastering another language.

7. You'll increase your fluency.

8. You'll enjoy German opera more when you understand the language.

9. You'll have a better understanding of German, Austrian, and Swiss culture.

10. You'll be one of the minority of people in the United States who know a second language.

Introduction

▶ This book presupposes that you already have begun learning German. You have learned basic vocabulary and grammar, but now you're ready to increase your German proficiency. That means practice.

Though this book is not a German grammar book, you will be provided with some grammatical clues that you need to remember. In fact, the exercises in this book are specifically designed to help you understand German grammar and, of course, to learn more German words. Each chapter deals with a part of German grammar, such as the article, the noun, the pronoun, and the preposition. It's best to begin with Part 1 and continue through the book without skipping sections, as each part builds on the one before.

Along with the written exercises, you will find other exercises on your audio CD. Listen to each exercise as many times as you like. Hearing the spoken words will greatly enhance your own understanding of the language. By listening to the German pronunciation and repeating the words yourself, you will acquire the language at a much more rapid pace.

Whether you are studying German in high school or college or learning it on your own, you will find that your proficiency provides all kinds of new opportunities. Wanting to take a trip to Germany? Maybe you are a transfer student to a German-speaking country. Or perhaps you want to be able to read German literature. It is incredible to read a work such as Goethe's *Faust* in the original.

Learning German will be fun and exciting. Not only are you learning another language, but also another country's culture and its way of defining and describing the world. This book provides you with the necessary practice to make your study worthwhile.

Part 1
The Article

A solid foundation on which to expand and practice German is a thorough knowledge of the German article and rules for its use. You should always have a good German phrase book and a German-to-English and English-to-German dictionary to help you if you have forgotten something. Also, online dictionaries such as *www.leo .org* or *www.foreignword.com* provide you with fast and correct answers.

The Attributive Adjective

The definite article is an adjective that has to agree in number (singular or plural), gender, and case with the noun that it modifies. There are three German definite articles that have to concur in number, gender, and case with the nouns they modify. All people, animals, and non-animated objects take a masculine, feminine, or neuter article. In order to be proficient in German, you must learn the correct article with each noun.

Exercise 1

The following nouns have the wrong definite articles. Provide the correct article and write the translation on the second line.

1. *das Vater* ....
2. *der Schule* ....
3. *die Schiff* ....
4. *der Mutter* ....
5. *die Kind* ....
6. *das Stuhl* ....

Exercise 2

Match the following German words with their English equivalents.

1. *Berg*   Greek

2. *Dampfer*   question

3. *Dreieck*   airplane

4. *Eisenbahn*   flesh

5. *Onkel*   earth

6. *Erde*   uncle

7. *Fleisch*   railroad

8. *Flugzeug*   triangle

9. *Frage*   steamer

10. *Grieche*   mountain

Exercise 3

Whatever the original gender, nouns become neuter when the suffixes *-chen* and *-lei* or *-lein* are attached. Words of affection and words expressing petiteness originate from the *-chen* and *-lein* endings. Keep in mind that the vowels *a*, *o*, *u*, and *au* change to *ä*, *ö*, *ü*, and *äu* when *-chen* or *-lein* are attached.

Circle the correct definite article before each noun and translate the words on the line that follows.

1. *(der, die, das) Männchen*   ....

2. *(der, die, das) Männlein*   ....

3. *(der, die, das) Fräulein*   ....

4. *(der, die, das) Karte*   ....

5. *(der, die, das) Frau*   ....

6. *(der, die, das) Mädchen*   ....

7. *(der, die, das) Mann*   ....

Three Genders and Four Cases

German nouns are either masculine, feminine, or neuter, and the article changes (but not always) with the four cases. The three genders and four cases assign a distinct role for the nouns in a sentence. The change in role of a noun is indicated in the change of the article. Pronouns also change with the four cases.

Exercise 4

TRACK 1

Listen to the track on the accompanying CD and repeat each singular noun with its definite article. Then, listen to the track again and translate into English what you hear. On the second line, specify whether it is the nominative, genitive, dative, or accusative case.

The following examples are definite articles with nouns in the singular. The first answer has been provided for you.

1. *der Mutter*   to, for the mother   dative

2. *das Mädchen*   ....

3. *den Vater*   ....

4. *das Mädchen*   ....

5. *die Mutter*   ....

6. *des Mädchens*   ....

7. *dem Vater*   ....

8. *der Vater*   ....

9. *dem Mädchen*   ....

10. *der Mutter*   ....

11. *die Mutter*   ....

12. *des Vaters*   ....

Exercise 5

Please translate the following words into English.

1. *Großmutter* ....

2. *Großvater* ....

3. *Kreis* ....

4. *Uhr* ....

5. *Stadt* ....

6. *Stier* ....

7. *Vetter* ....

8. *Winkel* ....

9. *Wissenschaft* ....

10. *Woche* ....

Exercise 6

You have to attach an *-s* to the genitive singular for most masculine nouns such as *des Haushalts* and all neuter nouns such as *des Kinderzimmers*.

In addition, you have to insert an *e* before the *-s* for one-syllable genitive masculine nouns such as *des Stuhles* and neuter: *des Buches.*

The same rule applies to nouns ending in *s* or *tz*—do not forget the *e.*

Translate and fill in the blanks, using *des* and one of the following words: *Mannes, Kindes, Schatzes, Fußes.*

1. of the treasure ....

2. of the foot ....

3. of the child ....

4. of the man ....

Exercise 7

With plural nouns, the three genders are not important. Instead the articles are all the same for all three genders in the nominative and accusative case.

The article is *die*. Make sure that you add an *n*-ending for all plural nouns in the dative, but if they already end in an *n*, you do not need to add an additional *n*.

Fill in the blanks with the correct form of the plural article and the translation.

1. Accusative: .... *Mädchen*   ....
2. Dative: .... *Mädchen*   ....
3. Genitive: .... *Mütter*   ....
4. Dative: .... *Müttern*   ....
5. Accusative: .... *Mütter*   ....
6. Nominative: .... *Mütter*   ....
7. Genitive: .... *Väter*   ....
8. Accusative: .... *Väter*   ....
9. Nominative: .... *Väter*   ....
10. Dative: .... *Vätern*   ....
11. Genitive: .... *Mädchen*   ....
12. Nominative: .... *Mädchen*   ....

Exercise 8

Translate the words on the short lines and then use the words in a sentence. Try to find the correct articles and be creative.

1. *Arbeit* ....

....

2. *Beispiel* ....

....

3. *Rock* ....

....

4. *Buch* ....

....

5. *Gabel* ....

....

6. *Geld* ....

....

7. *Freund* ....

....

8. *Glas* ....

....

9. *Kaffee* ....

....

10. *Kekse* ....

....

Cases in Action

The nominative case is the subject of a sentence, and the genitive case indicates possession. The dative case is the indirect object of a sentence. The accusative case is the direct object of a sentence. Note that the verb *sein* requires two nominatives! For example, in the sentence *Der Schriftsteller ist auch der Filmproduzent, Der Schriftsteller* is in the nominative case, as is *der Filmproduzent.* The sentence translates as "The writer is also the producer." You can only have two nominatives in a sentence if the verb is a form of "to be." With a different verb, you would find a nominative and an accusative or a dative case, as in: *Der Schriftsteller mag den Filmproduzent.* This sentence translates as "The writer likes the producer."

Exercise 9

Fill in the blanks to the left of the nouns with the correct articles in the proper case and then translate the sentences in the blanks. Hints: Question 1 pertains to the direct object, questions 2 and 3 pertain to the indirect object, the noun in question 4 is in the genitive case, question 5 pertains to the predicate noun, and the noun in question 6 is the subject of the sentence.

1. *Ich kaufte* .... *Hut.*

   ....

2. *Er kauft* .... *Vater einen Hut.*

   ....

3. *Die Frau gibt* .... *Sohn ein Stück Kuchen.*

   ....

4. *Der Bruder* .... *Vaters ist gekommen.*

....

5. *Herr Zimmermann ist* .... *Lehrer.*

....

6. .... *Vater wohnt in Berlin.*

....

A Unique Group of Modifiers

The next exercise follows the declension of the definite articles *der*, *die*, *das*. These words are called the *der*-words and include *dies-*, *jen-*, *jed-*, *welch-*, *solch-*, and *manch-*, the stems to which the respective endings are added. Take, for example, *den Mann* and *jeden Mann*. The endings for the articles are the same endings as the ones for the *der*-words.

Exercise 10

Match the six German *der*-words, *dies-*, *jen-*, *jed-*, *welch-*, *solch-*, and *manch-,* with their English equivalents. Choose one of the following: "that," "many (a)," "each," "which," "such (a)," and "this."

1. *welcher*   ....

2. *mancher*   ....

3. *dieser*   ....

4. *jeder*   ....

5. *solcher*   ....

6. *jener*   ....

Exercise 11

Choose the correct translation for each word.

1. *Leben* (death, life, lawn) ....

2. *Löffel* (spoon, knife, fork) ....

3. *Licht* (darkness, lever, light) ....

4. *Mensch* (man, mouse, month) ....

5. *Messer* (knife, measurement, radar) ....

6. *Milch* (tea, milk, juice) ....

7. *Schokolade* (strawberry, chocolate, desert) ....

8. *Tee* (tea, milk, juice) ....

9. *Teller* (saucer, plate, cup) ....

10. *Zucker* (sugar, pepper, salt) ....

Exercise 12

The following *der*-words are incorrectly declined. Correct them by declining them in the given case in the blanks to the left and then translate the words into English in the blanks to the right.

The answer to question 1 has been provided for you.

1. Nominative: *diese Mann*   *dieser*   this man

2. Dative: *diesen Frau*   ....

3. Accusative: *diese Kind*   ....

4. Accusative: *dieses Mann*   ....

5. Dative: *dieser Kind*   ....

6. Genitive: *dieser Mannes*   ....

7. Nominative: *dieser Frau*   ....

8. Accusative: *diesen Frau*   ....

9. Nominative: *diese Kind*   ....

10. Genitive: *diese Kind*   ....

11. Genitive: *diese Frau*   ....

12. Dative: *diesen Mann*   ....

Exercise 13

Translate the following words into English.

1. *die Wurst*   ....

2. *das Kalbfleisch*   ....

3. *das Lammfleisch*   ....

4. *das Rindfleisch*   ....

5. *der See*   ....

6. *der Schinken*   ....

7. *das Schweinefleisch*   ....

8. *der Staat*   ....

9. *die Umwelt*   ....

10. *der Vogel*   ....

Exercise 14

The plural *der*-word, *dies*-, endings are similar for all genders. Fill in the *der*-words, which are declined in the plural in the blanks to the left, and then translate them into English in the blanks to the right.

The first answer has been provided for you.

1. Nominative: *diese* .... *Männer* these men

2. Genitive: .... *Kinder* ....

3. Dative: .... *Kindern* ....

4. Dative: .... *Männern* ....

5. Accusative: .... *Männer* ....

6. Nominative: .... *Frauen* ....

7. Genitive: .... *Männer* ....

8. Nominative: .... *Kinder* ....

9. Genitive: .... *Frauen* ....

10. Dative: .... *Frauen* ....

11. Accusative: .... *Kinder* ....

12. Accusative: .... *Frauen* ....

Exercise 15

Translate the following words into English.

1. *die Fabrik* ....

2. *der Fisch* ....

3. *die Flasche* ....

4. *das Gemüse* ....

5. *das Gewicht* ....

6. *das Pfund* ....

7. *das Tier* ....

8. *das Wasser* ....

9. *der Wein* ....

10. *der Wissenschaftler* ....

Agreement with Nouns

Indefinite articles agree in number, gender, and case with the nouns they modify. The declension of the indefinite article (singular and plural) is similar to the *der*-words (*dieser,* and so on), except that you do not provide case endings to the masculine and neuter nominative singular and the neuter accusative singular.

Exercise 16

Fill in the blanks to the left with the correct word. Use either a form of *ein* + the appropriate ending or use a form of *kein* ("no," "not a") + the appropriate ending. Then translate into English in the blanks to the right.

The first answer has been provided for you.

1. Nominative: *ein*   *Mann*   a man

2. Accusative: .... *Männer* ....

3. Nominative: .... *Männer* ....

4. Dative: .... *Männern* ....

5. Dative: .... *Mann* ....

6. Genitive: .... *Mann(e)s* ....

7. Accusative: .... *Mann* ....

8. Genitive: .... *Männer* ....

Exercise 17

Translate the following words into English on the short line and then write a German sentence with the word in the long blank. Be correct and creative.

1. *bequem* ....

   ....

2. *braun* ....

   ....

3. *Erfindung* ....

   ....

4. *Farbe* ....

   ....

5. *Flüssigkeit* ....

   ....

6. *Forscher* ....

   ....

7. *hässlich* ....

   ....

8. *Idee* ....

   ....

9. *oben* ....

   ....

10. *Treppe* ....

    ....

Exercise 18

Fill in the blanks to the left with the correct indefinite article of the singular or negative plural of *eine Frau* (a woman). Then put the translation in the blanks to the right.

The first answer has been provided for you.

1.	Nominative:	*eine*	*Frau*	a woman
2.	Dative:	....	*Frauen*	....
3.	Nominative:	....	*Frauen*	....
4.	Accusative:	....	*Frauen*	....
5.	Genitive:	....	*Frauen*	....
6.	Dative:	....	*Frau*	....
7.	Accusative:	....	*Frau*	....
8.	Genitive:	....	*Frau*	....

Exercise 19

All examples of the indefinite article of the neuter *ein Kind* (a child) are incorrect. Correct them, then put the translation in the blanks to the right.

1. Accusative: *ein Kinder* ....
2. Genitive: *ein Kinder* ....
3. Dative: *eines Kindern* ....
4. Nominative: *einem Kinder* ....
5. Nominative: *keine Kind* ....
6. Accusative: *keine Kind* ....
7. Genitive: *keinen Kind(e)s* ....
8. Dative: *keiner Kind* ....

Exercise 20

Translate the following words into English.

1. *Anzug* ....
2. *Fahrstuhl* ....
3. *Kunst* ....
4. *Luft* ....
5. *Rolltreppe* ....
6. *Handtasche* ....
7. *Salz* ....
8. *Warenhaus* ....
9. *wirtschaftlich* ....
10. *wissenschaftlich* ....

Possessive Adjectives, Negations, and ein-words

Possessive adjectives, such as my (*mein*) and your (*dein*), follow the declension of *ein* and *kein* and are classified collectively as *ein*-words.

Exercise 21

Choose the correct translation for each word from the following words: its, her, your (polite singular and plural), their, my, a, his, our, no, your (familiar), and your (familiar plural).

The first question has been answered for you.

1. *sein* = its
2. *dein* ....
3. *ihr* ....
4. *sein* ....
5. *ein* ....
6. *mein* ....
7. *Ihr* ....
8. *kein* ....
9. *unser* ....
10. *euer* ....
11. *ihr* ....

Exercise 22

Match the following English words with their German equivalents.

1. warmth	*Angestellte*
2. process	*folgend*
3. clothing	*Größe*
4. rocket	*Mantel*
5. political party	*Leder*
6. leather	*Partei*
7. overcoat	*Rakete*
8. size	*Kleidung*
9. following	*Verfahren*
10. employee	*Wärme*

Exercise 23

Decline the *ein*-words in the masculine singular.
All of the answers to question 1 have been provided.

1. Nominative: *ein (kein, mein, dein, sein, ihr, unser, euer, ihr, Ihr) Mann*

2. Genitive: *eines, ..., meines, deines, ...,*

   ihres, ..., eu(e)res, ihres, ...,

   Mann(e)s

3. Dative: *einem, keinem, ..., deinem, seinem,*

   ...., unserem, eu(e)rem, ...,

   Ihrem, Mann

4. Accusative: *einen, keinen, meinen, ..., seinen, ihren,*

   unseren, ..., ihren, Ihren, Mann

Exercise 24

Decline the *ein*-words in the feminine singular.
All of the answers to question 1 have been provided for you.

1. Nominative: *eine (keine, meine, deine, seine, ihre, unsere, eu(e)re, ihre, Ihre) Frau*

2. Genitive: *einer, ..., meiner, ..., seiner,*

   ihrer, ..., eu(e)rer, ..., Ihrer, Frau

3. Dative: *einer, keiner, ..., deiner, ...,*

   ...., unserer, eu(e)rer, ihrer, ..., Frau

4. Accusative: *eine, ..., ..., ...,*

   ...., ..., ...,

   ...., ..., ..., Frau

Exercise 25

Translate the following words into English.

1. *die Aktenmappe*   ....

2. *die Buchhandlung*   ....

3. *der Handschuh*   ....

4. *die Hose*   ....

5. *die Jacke*   ....

6. *die Knöpfe* ....

7. *der Motor* ....

8. *das Oberhemd* ....

9. *der Sonnenschein* ....

10. *das Unterseeboot* ....

Exercise 26

Decline the *ein*-words in the neuter singular.
The answers to question 4 have been provided for you.

1. Nominative: *ein,* ...., ..., ...,

            ...., ..., ...,

            ...., ..., ..., *Kind*

2. Genitive: *eines, keines,* ...., ..., *seines,*

            ....,   *unseres,*   ....,   *ihres,*

            ...., *Kind(e)s*

3. Dative: *einem,* ...., *meinem, deinem,* ....,

            ihrem, ..., *eu(e)rem, ihrem,* ....,
            Kind

4. Accusative: *ein (kein, mein, dein, sein, ihr, unser, euer, ihr, Ihr) Kind*

Exercise 27

Decline the following *ein*-words in the plural.
Some of the answers have been provided.

1. Accusative: ....*Männer*

2. Dative: *keinen Männern*

3. Genitive: ....*Männer*

4. Nominative: *keine Männer*

5. Accusative: *keine Frauen*

6. Dative: ....*Frauen*

7. Genitive: *keiner Frauen*

8. Nominative: ....*Frauen*

9. Accusative: ....*Kinder*

10. Dative: ....*Kindern*

11. Genitive: ....*Kinder*

12. Nominative: ....*Kinder*

Exercise 28

Match the following German words with their English equivalents.

1. *Brief*   handkerchief
2. *frei*   people/nation
3. *Geschichte*   wash
4. *Schlips*   shoe
5. *Socke*   environment
6. *Schuh*   letter
7. *Umwelt*   free
8. *Volk*   history/story
9. *Wäsche*   necktie
10. *Taschentuch*   sock

Characteristics of Adjectives

Possessive adjectives are used to indicate possession or relationship. A possessive adjective agrees in gender, number, and case with the noun it modifies. Decline these adjectives similar to the indefinite article *ein* and its negative *kein*.

Exercise 29

TRACK 2

Listen to the track and repeat each word in German and then translate the words.

1. *mein* ....
2. *dein* ....
3. *sein* ....
4. *ihr* ....
5. *sein* ....
6. *unser* ....
7. *euer* ....
8. *ihr* ....
9. *Ihr* ....

Exercise 30

Translate the following words into English.

1. *billig*   ....
2. *Gesetz*   ....

3. *hart* ....

4. *heute* ....

5. *Klassenzimmer* ....

6. *neu* ....

7. *Sonne* ....

8. *Regen* ....

9. *teuer* ....

10. *weich* ....

Exercise 31

Translate each word below. The first answer has been provided for you.

1. *ich*   I

2. *du*   ....

3. *er*   ....

4. *sie*   ....

5. *es*   ....

6. *wir*   ....

7. *ihr*   ....

8. *sie*   ....

9. *Sie*   ....

Exercise 32

Translate the following words into English.

1. *breit*   ....

2. *eng*   ....

3. *geschichtlich*   ....

4. *Geschwindigkeit*   ....

5. *hoch*   ....

6. *niedrig*   ....

7. *offensichtlich*   ....

8. *Vorschrift*   ....

9. *Wien*   ....

10. *weit*   ....

Exercise 33

TRACK 3

The form of the possessive adjective needs to be consistent with the gender, number, and case of the noun that comes after it. Listen to the following sentences and repeat them out loud. Listen to them again and translate the following sentences into English in the blanks provided.

1. *Ich habe mein Heft.*

....

2. *Sie hat ihren Rucksack.*

....

3. *Wir lieben unsere Oma.*

....

4. *Unser Lehrer ist nicht hier.*

....

5. *Ich kenne Ihre Nachbarn nicht.*

....

Commonplace Usage

Dates, months, seasons, and the days of the week are preceded by the definite article in the proper declension.

Exercise 34

Translate the following examples. Some translations are from German to English while others are from English to German.

1. *Berlin, den 23. Juli, 6 . . .*

....

2. *Die Schule ist am (an + dem) Sonnabend geschlossen.*

....

3. Today is July 15th.

....

4. *Im (in + dem) Oktober ist es meistens kalt.*

....

5. We will go to the bakery on Monday.

....

Exercise 35

Translate the following words into English.

1. *Augenblick* ....

2. *Ausgang* ....

3. *Bevölkerung* ....

4. *Eingang* ....

5. *Gebiet* ....

6. *gleich* ....

7. *sozial* ....

8. *Stellung* ....

9. *Vorlesung* ....

10. *Zeit* ....

Exercise 36

With private possessions, parts of the body, and abstract nouns, you use the definite article when you have no doubt as to the possessor.

In each of the following sentences, translate the underlined words. Some translations are from German to English while others are from English to German.

1. *Sie wusch sich <u>ihre Hände</u>.*

....

2. He puts on <u>his hat</u>.

....

3. *Sie kämpfen für <u>die Freiheit</u>.*

....

4. <u>Life</u> is beautiful.

....

Exercise 37

Translate the following words into English.

1. *Entwicklung*   ....

2. *Ergebnis*   ....

3. *Gepäck*   ....

4. *Handkoffer*   ....

5. *Heimat*   ....

6. *Heimweh*   ....

7. *Jahrzehnt*   ....

8. *bald*   ....

9. *nun*   ....

10. *ruhig*   ....

Exercise 38

Use a definite article when you see an adjective in front of a proper name. Also use the definite article following the prepositions *in* ("in, into"), *nach* ("after"), *vor* ("before"), and *zu* ("to").

Translate the following phrases using the following words: little, poor, supper, school, *Frühstück*, and *Klein*. Some translations are from German to English while others are from English to German. This exercise practices the use of the definite article with prepositions.

1. before breakfast

   ....

2. *Sie sind in der Schule.*

   ....

3. for breakfast

   ....

4. *Nach dem Abendessen*

   ....

5. *der kleine Markus*

   ....

6. Fred is small.

   ....

7. *die arme Marie*

   ....

8. Stephanie is poor.

   ....

9. They go to school.

   ....

Exercise 39

Translate the following German words into English with words from the following list: table, strong, dining table, rapid/fast, bed, trip, war, solution, passport, red.

1. *Bett*   ....

2. *Fahrt*   ....

3. *Krieg*   ....

4. *Lösung*..

5. *Pass*   ....

6. *rot*   ....

7. *schnell*...

8. *stark*   ....

9. *Tafel*   ....

10. *Tisch*   ....

Exercise 40

Use the definite article with the names of streets, squares, and feminine and plural countries (note that countries are generally neuter in German). Use a definite article when it comes before the name of the country.

Translate the following examples.

1. *die Niederlande*   ....

2. *die Slowakei*   ....

3. *die Türkei*   ....

4. *die Vereinigten Staaten*   ....

5. *die Schweiz*   ....

Exercise 41

Translate the following words into English.

1. *Blitz* ....

2. *Blume* ....

3. *Donner* ....

4. *Gewitter* ....

5. *Geschäftswelt* ....

6. *Regen* ....

7. *schwierig* ....

8. *Welt* ....

9. *Wetter* ....

10. *zwischen* ....

Exercise 42

If nouns are of distinct genders, each must have its own definite or indefinite articles and possessive adjectives. Note that you have to put the definite article in front of the German word *meist* ("most").

Translate the following examples.

Some translations are from German to English while others are from English to German.

1. most people

....

2. the man and the woman

....

3. *mein Vater und meine Mutter*

....

Exercise 43

Choose the correct answer from the three words that follow.

1. *achte* (tenth, eighth, fifth) ....

2. *erste* (first, sixth, second) ....

3. *fünfte* (fourth, third, fifth) ....

4. *dritte* (second, first, third) ....

5. *neunte* (ninth, eleventh, fourth) ....

6. *sechste* (seventh, sixth, fifth) ....

7. *siebte* (seventh, sixth, fifth) ....

8. *Sturm* (stream, storm, tower) ....

9. *vierte* (fifth, fourth, eighth) ....

10. *Wolke* (cloud, world, stream) ....

11. *zehnte* (zero, tenth, third) ....

12. *zweite* (second, tenth, seventh) ....

Exercise 44

Don't use a definite article when you are making references to occupation, vocation, nationality, or situation, or when you use certain phrases, such as *Ich habe Kopfschmerzen*, which translates to "I have a headache."

Translate the following examples. Some translations are from German to English while others are from English to German.

1. *Meine Freundin ist Witwe.*

....

2. *Meine Mutter ist Amerikanerin.*

....

3. The young man is a student.

....

4. *Ich habe Kopfschmerzen (Zahnschmerzen).*

....

5. He is a good physician.

....

6. *Er ist Arzt.*

....

Exercise 45

Translate the following words into English.

1. *bald*   ....

2. *ehe*   ....

3. *geboren*   ....

4. *Gedächtnis*   ....

5. *Körper*   ....

6. *Notizbuch*   ....

7. *recht*   ....

8. *sobald*   ....

9. *trotz*   ....

10. *Treffpunkt*   ....

Part 2

The Noun

There are three declensions of nouns: strong, weak, and mixed. There are three classes in the strong declension. You do not have to attach an ending in the first class to construct the plural of the nominative singular, but you must attach an *e* in the second class to form the plural. In the third class, to construct the plural of the nominative, you must attach an *-er*.

The Class with No Endings: Class I

Class I of the strong declension comprises masculine and neuter nouns plus two feminine examples, *die Mutter* and *die Tochter*. Keep in mind that all masculine and neuter nouns ending in *-el, -en, -er* (along with neuter nouns with the prefix *ge-* and the suffix *-e*) make up Class I.

Exercise 1

When forming the plural, the Class I noun's stem vowel often changes from an *a* to *ä*, *o* to *ö*, *u* to *ü*, and *au* to *äu*. Do not attach an ending to the masculine noun except an *-n* in the dative plural.

There are errors in the following articles. Correct them. The first four questions are the masculine singular of father (*der Vater*) and questions 5–8 are the plural of father. Nom: stands for nominative case, Gen: for genitive, Dat: for dative, and Acc: for accusative.

1. Acc: *dem Vater*   ....

2. Dat: *den Vater*   ....

3. Gen: *der Vater*   ....

4. Nom: *des Vater*   ....

5. Acc: *der Vater*   ....

6. Nom: *der Vater*   ....

7. Dat: *die Vater*   ....

8. Gen: *den Vater*   ....

Exercise 2

In the first four questions, decline the masculine singular word for car (*der Wagen*), in questions 5–8, the plural of car.

1. Dat: *dem* ....
2. Nom: *der* ....
3. Acc: *den* ....
4. Gen: *des* ....
5. Dat: *den* ....
6. Acc: *die* ....
7. Nom: *die* ....
8. Gen: *der* ....

Exercise 3

In the first four questions, decline the neuter singular of girl (*das Mädchen*), in questions 5–8, the plural of girl.

1. Acc: *das* ....
2. Dat: *dem* ....
3. Gen: *des* ....
4. Nom: *das* ....
5. Dat: *den* ....
6. Acc: *die* ....
7. Nom: *die* ....
8. Gen: *der* ....

Exercise 4

In the first four questions, decline the masculine singular word for brother (*der Bruder*), in questions 5–8, the plural of brother.

1. Dat: *dem* ....
2. Acc: *den* ....
3. Gen: *des* ....
4. Nom: *der* ....
5. Dat: *den* ....
6. Acc: *die* ....
7. Gen: *der* ....
8. Nom: *die* ....

Exercise 5

In the first four questions, choose the correct declension for the masculine singular word for bird (*der Vogel*), in questions 5–8, for the plural of bird.

1. Acc: *den (Vogel, Vogels, Vögeln)* ....
2. Dat: *dem (Vogel, Vögeln, Vogels)* ....
3. Gen: *des (Vogels, Vögeln, Vogel)* ....
4. Nom: *der (Vogeln, Vogel, Vogels)* ....
5. Acc: *die (Vogels, Vögeln, Vögel)* ....
6. Dat: *den (Vogels, Vögeln, Vogel)* ....
7. Gen: *der (Vogels, Vögeln, Vögel)* ....
8. Nom: *die (Vogels, Vögeln, Vögel)* ....

Exercise 6

In the first four questions, decline the feminine singular word for mother (*die Mutter*), in questions 5–8, the plural of mother.

1. Acc: *die* ....

2. Gen: *der* ....

3. Nom: *die* ....

4. Dat: *der* ....

5. Acc: *die* ....

6. Gen: *der* ....

7. Dat: *den* ....

8. Nom: *die* ....

The Class with -e: Class II

The general rule for Class II nouns is to take the nominative singular of the noun and attach an *-e*. Except for neuter nouns, when you construct the plural you must add an umlaut to most nouns of Class II. However, you do not change the stem vowel to one with an umlaut in the plural for the German words *Tag*, *Jahr*, or *Monat*.

Class II includes masculine, neuter, and feminine nouns of more than one syllable ending in *-ig*, *-ing*, *-ling*, *-sal*, *-kunft*, and *-nis*. For this last group you are to double the *s* before the plural ending: *-isse*. And when the last component of compound nouns consists of a one-syllable noun, these are also Class II nouns.

Exercise 7

In the first four questions, decline the masculine singular word for son (*der Sohn*), in questions 5–8, the plural of son.

1. Acc: *den* ....
2. Nom: *der* ....
3. Gen: *des* ....
4. Dat: *dem* ....
5. Acc: *die* ....
6. Nom: *die* ....
7. Gen: *der* ....
8. Dat: *den* ....

Exercise 8

In the first four questions, decline the feminine singular word for night (*die Nacht*), in questions 5–8, the plural of night. Fill in the blanks using the following three words: *Nacht*, *Nächte*, and *Nächten*.

1. Acc: *die* ....
2. Nom: *die* ....
3. Gen: *der* ....
4. Dat: *der* ....
5. Dat: *den* ....
6. Acc: *die* ....
7. Gen: *der* ....
8. Nom: *die* ....

Exercise 9

In the first four questions, decline the feminine singular word for hand (*die Hand*), in questions 5–8, the plural of hand.

1. Acc: *die* ....

2. Dat: *der* ....

3. Gen: *der* ....

4. Nom: *die* ....

5. Acc: *die* ....

6. Dat: *den* ....

7. Nom: *die* ....

8. Gen: *der* ....

Exercise 10

In the first four questions, decline the masculine singular word for day (*der Tag*), in questions 5–8, the plural of day.

1. Gen: *des* ....

2. Nom: *der* ....

3. Acc: *den* ....

4. Dat: *dem* ....

5. Gen: *der* ....

6. Nom: *die* ....

7. Acc: *die* ....

8. Dat: *den* ....

Exercise 11

In the first four questions, decline the masculine singular word for month (*der Monat*), in questions 5–8, the plural of month. Some of the examples have mistakes. Find the mistakes and correct them.

1. Acc: *den Monat*   ....
2. Gen: *des Monat*   ....
3. Nom: *der Monat*   ....
4. Dat: *dem Monats*   ....
5. Dat: *den Monate*   ....
6. Acc: *die Monate*   ....
7. Gen: *der Monaten*   ....
8. Nom: *die Monate*   ....

Exercise 12

In the first four questions, decline the neuter singular word for year (*das Jahr*), in questions 5–8, the plural of year.

1. Acc: *das*   ....
2. Dat: *dem*   ....
3. Gen: *des*   ....
4. Nom: *das*   ....
5. Gen: *der*   ....
6. Acc: *die*   ....
7. Nom: *die*   ....
8. Dat: *den*   ....

The Class with -er: Class III

Remember that you have to attach -*er* to the nominative singular noun in order to construct the nominative plural. Also, you must attach an umlaut to the stem vowel.

Class III includes mostly one-syllable nouns, along with some masculine ones, and all nouns with the suffix -*tum*. Feminine nouns do not exist in Class III.

Exercise 13

Fill in the blanks with the correct singular nouns: *das Haus* ("house") for questions 1–4 and *das Land* ("land") for questions 5–8. Make sure you decline them accurately.

1. Gen: *des* ....
2. Dat: *dem* ....
3. Nom: *das* ....
4. Acc: *das* ....
5. Dat: *dem* ....
6. Acc: *das* ....
7. Nom: *das* ....
8. Gem: *des* ....

Exercise 14

There are errors in some of the following articles and nouns. Fill in the blanks with the correct plurals of *das Haus* for questions 1–4 and *das Land* for questions 5–8.

1. Acc: *die Häusern* ....
2. Nom: *die Häuser* ....
3. Dat: *der Häusern* ....
4. Gen: *den Häuser* ....
5. Acc: *der Länder* ....
6. Nom: *der Länder* ....
7. Gen: *der Länder* ....
8. Dat: *den Ländern* ....

Exercise 15

TRACK 4

Listen and translate these frequently used Class III neuter nouns.

1. *das Bild* ....
2. *das Feld* ....
3. *das Tal* ....
4. *das Gras* ....
5. *das Licht* ....
6. *das Volk* ....
7. *das Lied* ....
8. *das Dorf* ....

Exercise 16

Translate more of these significant Class III neuter and masculine nouns.

1. *der Ort* ....
2. *der Wald* ....
3. *das Kleid* ....
4. *das Wort* ....
5. *der Stern* ....
6. *das Nest* ....
7. *das Ei* ....
8. *das Schloss* ....

The Declension with No Modification

Since there is no alteration of the stem vowel, this declension is "weak." Construct the plural of all cases by attaching -*(e)n* to the nominative singular.

Exercise 17

Decline the singular of the feminine words *die Schule* ("school") for questions 1–4 and *die Tasche* ("bag") for questions 5–8.

Here's a hint: Feminine nouns never add an ending in the singular.

1. Acc: *die*   ....
2. Dat: *der*   ....
3. Gen: *der*   ....
4. Nom: *die*   ....
5. Acc: *die*   ....
6. Dat: *der*   ....
7. Gen: *der*   ....
8. Nom: *die*   ....

Exercise 18

Decline the plural of the feminine words *die Schule* (questions 1–4) and *die Tasche* (questions 5–8).

1. Gen: *der*   ....
2. Dat: *den*   ....
3. Acc: *die*   ....
4. Nom: *die*   ....
5. Gen: *der*   ....
6. Nom: *die*   ....
7. Acc: *die*   ....
8. Dat: *den*   ....

Exercise 19

Remember that some masculine nouns acquire an *-(e)n* ending in the singular and plural (with the exception of the nominative singular).

Decline the plural (questions 1–4) and singular (questions 5–8) forms of the word boy (*der Junge*).

1. Acc: *die* ....

2. Gen: *der* ....

3. Dat: *den* ....

4. Nom: *die* ....

5. Acc: *den* ....

6. Gen: *des* ....

7. Nom: *der* ....

8. Dat: *dem* ....

Exercise 20

Herr in front of a name (meaning "Mister") acquires the ending except in the nominative singular.

Decline the singular (questions 1–4) and plural (questions 5–8) forms for *der Herr.*

1. Nom: *der* ....
2. Gen: *des* ....
3. Dat: *dem* ....
4. Acc: *den* ....
5. Acc: *die* ....
6. Gen: *der* ....
7. Dat: *den* ....
8. Nom: *die* ....

Exercise 21

With the case and article shown, decline the word student (*der Student*).
Fill in the blanks using the words *Student* or *Studenten*.

1. Nom: *die* ....
2. Acc: *die* ....
3. Dat: *den* ....
4. Gen: *der* ....
5. Nom: *der* ....
6. Gen: *des* ....
7. Dat: *dem* ....
8. Acc: *den* ....

Exercise 22

Decline the singular forms (questions 1–4) and plural forms (questions 5–8) of the word philosopher (*der Philosoph*).

1. Nom: *der* ....

2. Gen: *des* ....

3. Dat: *dem* ....

4. Acc: *den* ....

5. Nom: *die* ....

6. Gen: *der* ....

7. Dat: *den* ....

8. Acc: *die* ....

Exercise 23

Translate the following masculine nouns ending in -*e* along with other masculine nouns with only one syllable.

1. *der Junge* ....

2. *der Narr* ....

3. *der Mensch* ....

4. *Herr Zimmermann ist mein Freund.*

....

5. *der Löwe* ....

6. *der Graf* ....

7. *Ich fahre mit Herrn Zimmermann nach Deutschland.*

....

8. *der Rabe* ....

The "Combo-Declension," or Mixed Declension

When you combine the strong and weak declensions, you get the combo-declension, or mixed declension. Nouns that acquire an *-s* in the genitive case singular are strong, while you attach an *-(e)n* for the plural in all four cases, making them weak. The plurals of these weak nouns do not acquire an umlaut.

Exercise 24

Mixed declensions have no feminine nouns. Decline the singulars (questions 1–4) and plurals (questions 5–8) of the word pain (*der Schmerz*).

1. Nom: *der* ....

2. Gen: *des* ....

3. Dat: *dem* ....

4. Acc: *den* ....

5. Nom: *die* ....

6. Gen: *der* ....

7. Dat: *den* ....

8. Acc: *die* ....

Exercise 25

Don't forget that the mixed declensions include no feminine nouns. The following singulars and plurals are of the word doctor (*der Doktor*). Choose the correct form for each word.

1. Dat: *den (Doktor, Doktors, Doktoren)*..
2. Acc: *den (Doktor, Doktors, Doktoren)*..
3. Gen: *der (Doktor, Doktors, Doktoren)*..
4. Acc: *die (Doktor, Doktors, Doktoren)*..
5. Gen: *des (Doktor, Doktors, Doktoren)*..
6. Nom: *der (Doktor, Doktors, Doktoren)*..
7. Dat: *dem (Doktor, Doktors, Doktoren)*..
8. Nom: *die (Doktor, Doktors, Doktoren)*..

Exercise 26

Decline the singulars and plurals of the word eye (*das Auge*).

1. Acc: *die*   ....
2. Dat: *den*   ....
3. Gen: *der*   ....
4. Nom: *die*   ....
5. Dat: *dem*   ....
6. Nom: *das*   ....
7. Acc: *das*   ....
8. Gen: *des*   ....

Exercise 27

Decline the singulars and plurals of the word study (*das Studium*).

1. Acc: *das* ....
2. Acc: *die* ....
3. Nom: *die* ....
4. Dat: *den* ....
5. Gen: *der* ....
6. Gen: *des* ....
7. Nom: *das* ....
8. Dat: *dem* ....

Exercise 28

Translate the following masculine and neuter nouns, some of which are derived from Greek or Latin.

1. *der Staat* ....
2. *das Drama (die Dramen)* ....
3. *das Datum (die Daten)* ....
4. *das Ohr* ....
5. *der Nachbar* ....
6. *das Gymnasium (die Gymnasien)* ....
7. *das Bett* ....
8. *der See* ....

9. *das Ende* ....

10. *der Bauer* ....

11. *das Hemd* ....

Unclassified Nouns

There are a small number of nouns that do not belong to Class I, Class II, or Class III. Even though they have to be declined like the weak declension in the singular, you have to attach an *-s* in the genitive singular as with strong nouns. These irregularly declined nouns are weak in the plural and end in *-(e)n*, but do not acquire an umlaut.

Exercise 29

The singular and plural of the word *der Glaube* ("belief") are used in the following examples. Some of the examples have mistakes in the nouns that you must find and correct.

1. Acc: *die Glaubens* ....

2. Dat: *den Glaubens* ....

3. Gen: *der Glauben* ....

4. Nom: *die Glaube* ....

5. Acc: *den Glauben* ....

6. Dat: *dem Glauben* ....

7. Gen: *des Glaube* ....

8. Nom: *der Glaubens* ....

Exercise 30

Decline the word *das Herz* ("heart") in the singular and plural.

1. Gen: *der*   ....
2. Nom: *die*   ....
3. Acc: *die*   ....
4. Dat: *den*   ....
5. Nom: *das*   ....
6. Dat: *dem*   ....
7. Gen: *des*   ....
8. Acc: *das*   ....

Exercise 31

Decline the word *der Wille* ("will") in the singular and plural.

1. Gen: *der*   ....
2. Dat: *dem*   ....
3. Nom: *der*   ....
4. Acc: *die*   ....
5. Gen: *des*   ....
6. Acc: *den*   ....
7. Nom: *die*   ....
8. Dat: *den*   ....

Exercise 32

Decline the word *der Gedanke* ("thought") in the singular and plural.

1. Nom: *die* ....
2. Dat: *den* ....
3. Gen: *der* ....
4. Acc: *die* ....
5. Dat: *dem* ....
6. Gen: *des* ....
7. Nom: *der* ....
8. Acc: *den* ....

Exercise 33

Attach an *-s* to the nominative to create all plurals of foreign words—which are strong singular nouns. Keep in mind that you are not to attach the *-n* in these plurals.

Practice making plurals from the singulars of the following nouns. The left column is the singular. Fill in the blanks with the correct plural.

1. Nom: *das Hotel* ....
2. Nom: *das Piano* ....
3. Nom: *das Auto* ....
4. Nom: *das Kino* ....

Essential Elements of Nouns

There are five different plural endings. The nominative singular, genitive singular, and nominative plural are the three principal parts of the noun. In order to master the German language, you must know the principal parts of the most frequently used nouns.

Exercise 34

Questions 1–3 are in the nominative singular, questions 4–6 are in the genitive singular, and questions 7–9 are the nominative plural.

Practice translating from English into German the three principal parts of the following nouns. Match the English words with their German equivalents.

1. the child	*die Männer*
2. the man	*die Kinder*
3. the woman	*die Frauen*
4. of the woman	*der Frau*
5. of the child	*des Kind(e)s*
6. of the man	*der Mann*
7. the children	*die Frau*
8. the men	*das Kind*
9. the women	*des Mannes*

Nouns as Specific Things

When a name specifies a particular river, city, country, person, etc., it is a proper noun. In colloquial German, proper names have an *-s* ending in the genitive case, with no apostrophe. However, you must omit the *-s* and use an apostrophe after the noun when that proper noun concludes in a sibilant (*-s, -sch, -ss, -z, -tz, -x*).

Exercise 35

Translate the following sentences into English.

1. *Karls Freundin ist in Deutschland.*

    ....

2. *Hans' Schwester macht eine Reise durch Deutschland.*

    ....

3. *Maries Hut liegt auf dem Tisch.*

    ....

4. *Georgs Vater kommt heute nicht.*

    ....

5. *Fritz' und Max' Vater wohnt in München.*

    ....

Exercise 36

With place names, you sometimes utilize the genitive *-s*. If you are using the preposition "*von*" instead of the genitive, though, you do not need to change the noun. Make sure that you do not attach an *-s* to the noun in the genitive when an adjective comes before the proper noun.

Translate the German into English.

1. *Goethes Werke*   ....

2. *der Sohn der alten Frau Hausmann*

    ....

3. *die Häuser von London*   ....

4. *die Werke des jungen Frost*   ....

5. *die Länder Europas*   ....

6. *Frau Werkmeisters Sohn*   ....

7. *Europas Dichter*   ....

8. *die großen Städte von China*

....

Exercise 37

TRACK 5

Make sure that you put a proper noun in the genitive when a title is used with the proper name. When an article comes before the proper noun, do not change it. You must, however, add a genitive -*s* to the title even if a name doesn't follow the title. The following examples clarify this point.

Listen to the German phrases and sentences and translate them into English.

1. *Doktor Wengers Tochter*

....

2. *die Tochter des Doktor Wenger*

....

3. *die Tochter des Doktors*

....

4. *Königin Viktorias Feldzug*

....

5. *der Feldzug der Königin Viktoria*

....

6. *der Feldzug der Königin*

....

7. *Maximilian der Große lebte im 7. Jahrhundert.*

....

8. *Der Sohn Maximilian des Großen war Roland der Fromme.*

....

9. *Sie kämpften mit Maximilian dem Großen.*

....

10. *Sie sprechen über Maximilian den Großen.*

....

Masculine, Feminine, and Neuter Nouns

Virtually every noun that concludes in *-en* (other than nouns that come from the infinitive) is masculine. Nouns are masculine when they end in *-er*, denoting an instrument, tool, or person (other than *die Mutter*).

Exercise 38

Some of the following examples are in German and some are in English.

Match each example with its correct translation.

1. the teacher   *der Faden*
2. the artist   *der Laden*
3. *der Garten*   the gardener
4. *der Hammer*   the garden
5. the store   *der Künstler*
6. *der Boden*   the hammer
7. the thread   *der Lehrer*
8. *der Norden*   the north
9. *der Gärtner*   the floor

Exercise 39

Nouns are always masculine when they have the endings *-ig*, *-ich*, *-ling*, and *-mus*, and the times of the day, days of the week, months, and seasons (other than *die Nacht*) are also masculine.

Translate the following English and German words.

1. *der Nachmittag* ....

2. (the) Monday ....

3. (the) May ....

4. the king ....

5. the rug ....

6. *der Abend* ....

7. *der Käfig* ....

8. *der Frühling* ....

9. *der Nationalismus* ....

10. (the) idealism ....

11. the novice ....

12. *der Sommer* ....

13. the morning ....

Exercise 40

TRACK 6

Most nouns that end in *-e* are feminine (other than nouns denoting masculine beings and a few neuters). Nouns are also feminine (and are part of the weak declension) when you add the *-ei*, *-heit*, *-keit*, *-in*, *-ion*, *-tion*, *-schaft*, *-tät*, and *-ung* suffixes.

Listen and translate the German into English and the English into German.

1. *die Schule* ....

2. the rose ....

3. *die Bäckerei* ....

4. the religion ....

5. *die Freundin* ....

6. (the) bravery ....

7. *die Universität* ....

8. the newspaper ....

9. *die Verwandschaft* ....

10. the beauty ....

11. *die Nation* ....

Exercise 41

Objects that express petiteness are always neuter when you construct them with the suffixes *-chen* and *-lein*. Note that all nouns coming from infinitives are neuter as are those that conclude with *-um* and *-ium*. All metals are neuter.

Fill in the blanks using the following words: (the) copper, the girl, (the) gold, the paper, (the) silver, the little dog, the study, the singing, the date, the writing, and the dancing.

1. *das Singen* ....

2. *das Silber* ....

3. *das Tanzen* ....

4. *das Kupfer* ....

5. *das Mädchen* ....

6. *das Studium* ....

7. *das Papier* ....

8. *das Gold* ....

9. *das Schreiben* ....

10. *das Hündchen* ....

11. *das Datum* ....

Compound Nouns

Compound nouns, meaning two nouns put together to form a new noun, are frequently used in the German language. *Kindergarten* is an example of a compound noun: The nouns are *Kinder* and *Garten*. The meaning of these compound nouns can easily be guessed if you know the meaning of the two nouns that make up the compound noun. Sometimes the compound noun has a different meaning than the two individual nouns, as is the case with the word *Handschuh*. Although *Hand* translates to "hand," and *Schuh* is "shoe," the compound noun translates as "glove." The second noun in a compound noun such as *Handschuhe* ("gloves") determines the noun's meaning and article. The first noun in a compound noun is merely a modifier.

Exercise 42

Fill in the blanks.
The third answer has been provided for you.

1. .... (*das Haus* ["the house"] + *der Herr* ["the master"] = the master of the house

2. *Der Badezimmerschlüssel* =

....

3. *das Schlafzimmer* (*der Schlaf* ["the sleep"] + *das Zimmer* ["the room"]) = the bedroom

4. *die Hafergrütze* =

....

The Nominative Case in Action

Keep in mind that the nominative case is the subject of a sentence and governs the predicate nominative following the verb *sein* (to be).

Exercise 43

Translate the following sentences.

1. *Er ist der Freund meines Bruders.*

....

2. *Das Baby ist ein Mädchen.*

....

3. *Der Graf hat kein Geld.*

....

The Genitive Case in Action

Remember that you communicate possession with the genitive case, to indicate "of the," "of my," etc. Instead of the genitive forms, *von* is commonly utilized in connection with cities and countries, following distinct prepositions, and in communicating indefinite time.

Exercise 44

TRACK 7

Listen to the following German sentences and translate them into English.

1. *Die Mutter der Kinder ist in der Schweiz.*

   ....

2. *Der Kollege meiner Schwester heißt Michael.*

   ....

3. *Madrid ist die Hauptstadt von Spanien.*

   ....

4. *Der Flughafen von Frankfurt ist sehr bekannt.*

   ....

5. *Trotz seiner Prüfung geht er ins Rockkonzert.*

   ....

6. *Eines Tages rief er uns an.*

   ....

7. *Eines Abends trat er in meine Wohnung.*

   ....

The Dative Case in Action

If you want to express that something is done for somebody or something, you use the dative case and an indirect object. Take, for example, the sentence "Ernst gives his mother a book." The person doing the action, Ernst, is in the nominative. The recipient, or beneficiary of the action—in this case "the mother"—is in the dative case, and the direct object in this case "the book"—is in the accusative case.

There are also so-called dative prepositions, after which you must use the dative case. These prepositions are *aus* ("from, out of"), *bei* ("near, with"), *nach* ("to, after"), *von* ("from") and *zu* (which, like *nach*, also means "to," but indicates movement toward a place or a person). Dative prepositions are used with neuter names of cities and countries.

Exercise 45

Match the following sentences with their correct English translation.

1. *Jens kam aus seinem Zimmer.* The doctor is with the patient.

2. *Jens arbeitet bei McDonalds.* We'll go to the beach today.

3. *Der Doktor ist bei der Patientin.* The teacher talks to him.

4. *Die Lehrerin spricht mit ihm.* We'll go to Salzburg tomorrow.

5. *Wir fahren morgen nach Salzburg.* Jens came from his room.

6. *Jens kommt gerade vom Markt zurück.* Jens works at McDonald"s.

7. *Wir fahren heute zum Strand.* Jens is just returning from the market.

Exercise 46

TRACK 8

You utilize the dative case as the lone object following the so-called dative verbs, examples of which follow.

Listen and translate the German into English and English into German.

1. *antworten* ....

2. to follow ....

3. *gleichen* ....

4. to meet ....

5. *gefallen* ....

6. to help ....

7. *danken* ....

8. to belong to ....

9. *passen* ....

10. to serve ....

11. *gehorchen* ....

12. to harm ....

The Accusative Case in Action

The accusative case governs the direct object in a sentence. There are several accusative prepositions after which you have to use the accusative case. The most frequently used are: *bis* ("till, until, by"), *durch* ("through"), *für* ("for") *gegen* ("against"), *ohne* ("without") and *um* ("around").

Exercise 47

Match each German example with its English equivalent.

1. *Ich bin bis Ende August in Stuttgart.*
2. *Wir gingen ohne unseren Bruder ins Theater.*
3. *Wir sind durch die Stadt gelaufen.*
4. *Hier ist ein Brief für dich.*
5. *Die ganze Welt ist gegen mich.*
6. *Ich kümmere mich um dich.*

We went to the theater without our brother.

I'll be in Stuttgart till the end of August.

Here is a letter for you.

The whole world is against me.

We walked through town.

I will take care of you.

Exercise 48

Most time expressions that do not include a preposition are in the accusative case. Phrases and greetings such as *Gute Nacht!* are part of that. The adjective *gut* gets an accusative ending, because it is a time expression. Seeing the complete sentence should clarify this: *Ich wünsche dir eine gute Nacht.*

Translate the German into English and the English into German.

1. Good night!

   ....

2. *Herzlichen Gruß!*

   ....

3. *Sie sind schon einen Monat in Südamerika.*

   ....

4. *Guten Morgen!*

   ....

5. We worked (have worked) all day.

   ....

6. *Diesen Winter fahre ich nach Amerika.*

   ....

E Part 3
The Pronoun

As it does in English, the German pronoun replaces a noun and refers to persons or things understood by the context. One way in which the German pronoun differs from the English is that the German equivalents of he and she not only refer to people, but also to things. Thus, the pronoun to use for the Geman word for milk, *die Milch*, is *sie* ("she").

Pronouns: Gender

There are three genders of personal pronouns: the masculine *er* ("he"), the feminine *sie* ("she"), and the neuter *es* ("it").

The endings of the third person singular and plural are similar to the equivalent case endings of the definite article. So the nominative pattern is *der–er, die–sie, das–es*. Accusative: *den–ihn, die–sie, das–es*. Dative: *dem–ihm, der–ihr, dem–ihm, der–ihr, den–ihnen*, etc.

The pronoun "you" has three equivalents in German:

1. The *du* form (the familiar form in the singular) is used when you speak to a pet, a close friend, a child, or a member of the family.
2. When you speak to more than one person informally, use *ihr*, the plural of *du*.
3. When you speak to people you know only slightly or to people you do not know at all (either singular or plural) use *Sie* (the so-called formal address).

Before you change the form *Sie* to *du*, you must have a very private or close relationship with the person you are addressing. Use *Sie* if you are not sure which to use.

Exercise 1

Translate the declension of singular personal pronouns.

1. Third Person Acc: *ihn*   ....   *sie*   ....

    es   ....

2. First Person Gen: *(meiner)*   ....

3. Second Person Dat: *dir*   ....

4. First Person Nom: *ich*   ....

5. Second Person Acc.   *dich*   ....

6. Second Person Nom: *du*   ....

7. Third Person Nom: *er*   ....   *sie*   ....

                                                          es   ....

8. First Person Acc.   *mich*   ....

9. Second Person Gen: (*deiner*)   ....

10. First Person Dat: *mir*   ....

11. Third Person Gen: *seiner*   ....   *ihrer*   ....

                                                           seiner   ....

12. Third Person Dat.   *ihm*   ....   *ihr*   ....

                                                           ihm   ....

Exercise 2

Translate the declension of plural personal pronouns.

1. Second Person Acc: *euch*   ....

2. Second Person Dat: *euch*   ....

3. Third Person Gen: *ihrer*   ....

                                                           Ihrer (polite)   ....

4. First Person Nom: *wir*   ....

5. Third Person Acc: *sie*   ....

                                                           Sie (polite)   ....

6. Second Person Nom: *ihr* ....

7. First Person Acc: *uns* ....

8. Third Person Nom: *sie* ....

   Sie (polite form) ....

9. First Person Gen: *(unser)* ....

10. Second Person Gen: *(euer)* ....

11. First Person Dat: *uns* ....

12. Third Person Dat: *ihnen* ....

    Ihnen (polite) ....

Exercise 3

You must modify the structure of the pronoun so that it agrees with the gender, case, and number of the noun it replaces. Pronouns are affected by the same rules as the nouns for which they stand.

Some of the sentences have mistakes. Write the correct sentences on the lines.

1. *Er grüßt sie.*

   ....

2. *Die Vater grüßt das Frau.*

   ....

3. *Sie geht mit ihm.*

   ....

4. *Der Sohn geht mit die Vater.*

   ....

Exercise 4

TRACK 9

Listen to and translate the following German sentences. Each pronoun refers to a noun in the sentence above it.

1. *Der Teppich ist rot.*

....

2. *Er ist rot.*

....

3. *Der Vater sieht die Uhr.*

....

4. *Er sieht sie.*

....

5. *Die Frau gibt dem Kind einen Teddybären.*

....

6. *Sie gibt ihn ihm.*

....

Exercise 5

The grammatical gender, rather than the natural gender, determines the gender of the corresponding pronoun. An exception is that when you substitute a pronoun for *das Mädchen,* you use the feminine form of the personal pronoun, even though this word is of neuter gender.

Read the sentences out loud and then match each sentence with its correct translation.

1. *Kennen Sie das Mädchen?*	They are speaking with the boy.
2. *Kennen Sie sie?*	They are speaking with him.
3. *Sie sprechen mit dem Jungen.*	Do you know her?
4. *Sie sprechen mit ihm.*	Do you know the girl?

Pronominal Compounds

Pronominal compounds are the only exceptions to the usual principle that the pronoun (whether it refers to a person or an object) concurs with the grammatical gender, number, and case of the noun it replaces.

Use *da-* instead of the proper pronoun. The preposition is compounded with this particle: *davon, damit*, etc. These compounds cannot refer to people.

Exercise 6

TRACK 10

Listen to and translate the following German sentences.

1. *Sie schreibt mit dem Filzstift.*

   ....

2. *Sie schreibt damit.*

   ....

3. *Die Schüler spielen mit den Tennisbällen.*

   ....

4. *Sie spielen damit.*

   ....

5. *Sie wussten von der Relativitätstheorie.*

   ....

6. *Sie wussten davon.*

   ....

7. *Er sitzt auf dem Sofa.*

   ....

8. *Er sitzt darauf.*

   ....

9. *Sie hat die Handtasche.*

   ....

10. *Sie hat sie.*

   ....

Exercise 7

When constructing a pronominal compound, you have to insert an *r* between the *da-* and the preposition, if the preposition starts with a vowel.

The words in each following sentence are scrambled. Rewrite the sentences correctly in the first blanks and then translate the sentences in the second blanks.

1. *Fahrt denken sie die schöne an.* ....

   ....

2. *denken daran sie.* ....

   ....

3. *sie den an denken Freund.* ....

   ....

4. *sie ihn denken an.* ....

   ....

Reflexive Pronouns

Reflexive pronouns are in the accusative case; they are direct objects referring back to the subject. For example, *sich* (an accusative reflexive pronoun) is both third person singular and plural.

Exercise 8

Notice that some reflexive verbs are weak, some are strong. Translate the German to English.

1. *Sie freuen sich* ....
2. *wir freuen uns* ....
3. *sie freuen sich* ....
4. *sich freuen* ....
5. *ihr freut euch* ....
6. *ich freue mich* ....
7. *er freut sich* ....
8. *du freust dich* ....

Exercise 9

Each example is scrambled. Correct each and then translate the German to English.

1. *waschen sich Sie* ....
2. *sie sich waschen* ....
3. *uns waschen wir* ....
4. *wasche ich mich* ....
5. *waschen sich* ....
6. *wäschst dich du* ....
7. *sich er wäscht* ....
8. *ihr euch wascht* ....

Exercise 10

Verbs are frequently used reflexively.
Translate the following German into English.

1. *sich interessieren* ....

2. *sich freuen* ....

3. *sich setzen* ....

Verbs, Pronouns, and the Dative Case

Intransitive verbs coming after the dative case demand reflexive pronouns in the dative. The exception is when the accusative *sich* is used in the structures of the third person (singular and plural). Translate *sich helfen* as "to help oneself."

Exercise 11

Fill in the blanks with the correct form of *helfen,* either *helfe, helfen, hilfst, helft,* or *hilft,* and then translate the German phrases into English.

1. *sie* .... *sich* ....

2. *Sie* .... *sich* ....

3. *er* .... *sich* ....

4. *wir* .... *uns* ....

5. *ich* .... *mir* ....

6. *du* .... *dir* ....

7. *ihr* .... *euch* ....

Exercise 12

In the dative case, only *mir* and *dir* are unlike the other reflexive pronouns. Keep in mind that you are frequently communicating possession with the reflexive pronouns, since you often translate the dative case, *mir*, *dir*, etc., by "for me," "to me," etc.

Underline all of the verbs and then translate the following German sentences.

1. *Ihr wascht euch die Socken.*

   ....

2. *Sie waschen sich die Socken.*

   ....

3. *Sie waschen sich die Socken.*

   ....

4. *Ich wasche mir die Socken.*

   ....

5. *Er wäscht sich die Socken.*

   ....

6. *Du wäschst dir die Socken.*

   ....

7. *Wir waschen uns die Socken.*

   ....

Exercise 13

Examine and compare the following two sentences, then translate them.

1. *Sie kauft ihr eine Bluse.*

   ....

2. *Sie kauft sich eine Bluse.*

   ....

Pronouns: Reciprocal

Selbst and *einander* are the two reciprocal pronouns (not reflexive pronouns). You do not decline them. If you want to stress a truth or declaration, you use *selbst* (herself, himself, themselves, etc.). Translate *einander* as "each other." Make sure that you do not decline *selbst* and *einander,* since they are not reflexive pronouns and never change their form.

Exercise 14

Unscramble the following sentences. Then translate them.

1. *machen Mittagessen das sich Sie.*

   ....

   ....

2. *oft sehen sich Sie.*

   ....

   ....

3. *das sie Mittagessen machen selbst sich.*

   ....

   ....

4. *sie selbst es gesagt hat.*

   ....

   ....

Possessive Pronouns

You may use possessive adjectives as possessive pronouns; you inflect them like the *ein*-words. Attach endings to the masculine nominative singular, neuter nominative singular, and neuter accusative singular when they are used as pronouns.

Exercise 15

Translate the following German sentences and then underline each verb.

1. *Nehmen Sie meinen Pullover! Danke, ich habe meinen.*

   ....

2. *Ihr Büro ist größer als unsers.*

   ....

3. *Sie braucht ihren Bleistift und ich meinen.*

   ....

4. *Er schreibt mit seiner Feder und sie schreibt mit ihrer.*

   ....

5. *Ist das Ihr Regenschirm, Herr Werkmeister? Nein, das ist nicht meiner, es ist Ihrer.* ....

   ....

6. *Wessen Kind ruft sie, seins oder Ihrs?*

   ....

Demonstrative Pronouns

Emphatic or demonstrative pronouns are used instead of nouns. *Dieser* (this one) pertains to a person, thing, idea, or an item that is close to the speaker. *Jener* (that one) pertains to a person or thing that is at a greater distance from the speaker.

Exercise 16

The following sentences have mistakes concerning *dieser* and *jener*. Correct them on the short line and then translate the following German sentences on the long line.

1. *War es dieses Restaurant? Nein, es war jener.* ....

    ....

2. *Dieses Geschäftshaus ist hoch, jene ist nicht so hoch.* ....

    ....

3. *Dieses hat es nicht getan, aber jenes.* ....

    ....

Exercise 17

Just as you declined the demonstrative pronouns *dieser* and *jener,* you inflect definite articles similarly when they are used as relative pronouns. Also, note that *dies* and *das* remain unchanged at the front of a sentence when you use them as demonstratives.

Read the sentences out loud and then translate them.

1. *Der hat es nicht getan.*

....

2. *Denen ist nicht zu helfen.*

....

3. *Das sind meine Kusinen.*

....

4. *Dies ist mein Schüler.*

....

5. *Dem kann ich das nicht geben.*

....

Exercise 18

Derselbe ("the same") is a compound of the definite article *der* and *selbe* ("same"). *Selbe* acquires the weak adjective declension, with the initial portion of the compound being declined similar to the definite article. You are to decline the rarely used *derjenige* (he who) just as you decline *derselbe*.

Decline the following. The answers for the nominative singular and plural for all genders have been provided.

1. Acc. Plural: ....

2. Nom. Neuter Singular: *dasselbe*

3. Nom. Plural: *dieselben*

4. Gen. Neuter Singular: ....

5. Dat. Plural: ....

6. Dat. Neuter Singular: ....

7. Gen. Plural: ....

8. Nom. Masculine: Singular: *derselbe*

9. Acc. Masculine Singular: ....

10. Gen. Masculine Singular: ....

11. Nom. Feminine Singular: *dieselbe*

12. Dat. Masculine Singular: ....

13. Dat. Feminine Singular: ....

14 Gen. Feminine Singular: ....

15. Acc. Neuter Singular: ....

16. Acc. Feminine Singular: ....

Asking Questions

When you make an inquiry, you have to use question words, also known as interrogative pronouns. The case endings of the definite article (*der, die, das*) must agree with the case endings of interrogative pronouns.

Exercise 19

There is no genitive or dative form in the neuter.
Translate the following.

1. *Wem haben Sie den Kuchen gegeben?*

....

2. *Was hat er Ihnen gestern gesagt?*

....

3. *Mit wem sprechen Sie?*

....

4. *Wen sehen Sie?* ....

5. *Wessen Klavier ist das?* ....

6. Masculine and Feminine Gen: *wessen* ....

7. Masculine and Feminine Nom: *wer* ....

8. Masculine and Feminine Dat: *wem* ....

9. Neuter Nom: *was* ....

10. Masculine and Feminine Acc: *wen* ....

11. *Wer ist das?* ....

12. Neuter Acc: *was* ....

Exercise 20

Translate inquiries pertaining to an object, an idea, or an event as "of what," "with what," "on what," etc., (using *wovon, womit, worauf,* etc.). Also, be sure to use the interrogative *wo* with the correct preposition in each case. Just as with the pronominal compounds with *da-,* set an *r* in the middle of *wo* and the preposition in order to support pronunciation if the preposition starts with a vowel. Examples are: *worauf, woran,* and *worin.*

The words in each sentence are out of order. Put them together into sentences and then translate the resulting set of questions and answers.

1. *wem Mit Sie sprechen? Ich mit meinem Mechaniker spreche.*

....

2. *Sie Wovon sprachen? Wir Drama dem sprachen neuen von.*

....

3. *An denken wen Sie? meine Ich Schweden denke an in Tochter.*

....

4. *Sie Woran denken? Ich den denke gestrigen schönen Tag an.*

....

Asking "What kind of . . . ?"

In the question words *was für* ("what kind of"), *für* has no prepositional force and does not influence *ein* or the next noun. You remove *ein* when the following noun is plural.

Exercise 21

For each of the following, choose the correct *ein*-word and fill in the blank. Then translate the sentences.

1. *Was für Briefumschläge haben Sie da?*

   ....

2. *Was für* .... *Mädchen ist sie?* (einem, ein, einen)

   ....

3. *Mit was für* .... *Zug fahren Sie?* (einen, einem, ein)

   ....

Referring to Antecedents

You make a connection between a sentence and a relative sentence by using a relative pronoun. Here is an example: *Der Mann, dessen Schwester ich gestern gesehen habe, ist jetzt in der Bücherei.* This translates as: "The man, whose sister I saw yesterday, is now in the library." The part "whose sister I saw yesterday" is the relative clause, introduced by the relative pronoun "whose."

In German, this relative pronoun needs to agree in number and gender with the noun that comes before it.

The case of the relative pronoun, however, is determined by its grammatical significance in the relative clause. In the above mentioned example, "whose" translates as *dessen* and is in the genitive case.

Exercise 22

Translate the following relative pronouns into English.

1. Acc. Neuter Singular: *das* ....
2. Gen. Neuter Singular: *dessen* ....
3. Dat. Neuter Singular: *dem* ....
4. Acc. Plural: *die* ....
5. Dat. Feminine Singular: *der* ....
6. Acc. Feminine Singular: *die* ....
7. Acc. Masculine Singular: *den* ....
8. Dat. Plural: *denen* ....
9. Nom. Masculine Singular: *der* ....
10. Nom. Neuter Singular: *das* ....
11. Nom. Feminine Singular: *die* ....
12. Gen. Masculine Singular: *dessen* ....
13. Gen. Plural: *deren* ....
14. Nom. Plural: *die* ....
15. Dat. Masculine Singular: *dem* ....
16. Gen. Feminine Singular: *deren* ....

Exercise 23

TRACK 11

Listen to and translate the following German sentences.

1. *Die Frau, die dort steht, heißt Kühn.*

....

2. *Der Mann, dessen Sohn ich kenne, wohnt hier.*

....

3. *Das ist das Kind, dem sie den Ring gegeben hat.*

....

4. *Der Mantel, den er heute trägt, ist neu.*

....

5. *Der Spiegel, an dem er steht, gehört mir.*

....

6. *Die Männer, mit denen ich gestern gesprochen habe, sind meine Mitstudenten.*

....

7. *Der Junge, der das Lesen heute nicht beenden kann, muss morgen wiederkommen.*

....

Exercise 24

Always use commas to set off the relative clause from the main clause, and never leave out the relative pronoun. *Welch* (which) is an additional relative pronoun.

Decline *welch* according to the given number, gender, and case. Since *welch* does not have genitive forms, *dessen* and *deren* are used in that case. Some of the answers have been provided.

1. Acc. Masc. Singular: *welchen*

2. Gen. Plural: ....

3. Dat. Fem. Singular: ....

4. Acc. Neut. Singular: ....

5. Acc. Plural: ....

6. Nom. Masc. Singular: *welcher*

7. Acc. Fem. Singular: ....

8. Nom. Plural: ....

9. Nom. Fem. Singular: ....

10. Gen. Fem. Singular: ....

11. Nom. Neut. Singular: ....

12. Gen. Neut. Singular: ....

13. Gen. Masc. Singular: *dessen*

14. Dat. Plural: ....

15. Dat. Masc. Singular: *welchem*

16. Dat. Neut. Singular: ....

Exercise 25

Question words such as *was, wer, wessen, wen,* and *wem* can also be used as relative pronouns. The relative pronoun *was* is used very frequently when the antecedent is an indefinite pronoun such as *etwas* ("something") or a superlative such as "the most beautiful."

Match each of questions 2, 5, 6, 8, 9, and 10 with one of the following sets of words (he who, whoever), (what, whatever, that), (whose), (whomever, to whom), (whomever/whom). Then translate questions 1, 3, 4, 7, and 11.

1. *Das ist das Schönste, was ich je gehabt habe.*

   ....

2. Acc: *was* ....

3. *Was ich habe, gehört dir.*

   ....

4. *Wer einmal lügt, dem glaubt man nicht.*

   ....

5. Nom: *was* ....

6. Nom: *wer* ....

7. *Alles, was sie darüber gehört hat, stimmt.*

   ....

8. Acc: *wen* ....

9. Gen: *wessen* ....

10. Dat: *wem* ....

11. *Wem ich glauben soll, weiß ich nicht.*

....

Three Classes of Pronouns

German has three classes of indefinite pronouns. You do not decline a few indefinite pronouns, you partially decline some, and others have a complete declension.

Exercise 26

TRACK 12

Use the pronoun *man* ("one, they, people") in the singular. In German, adjectives are frequently changed into neuter adjectival nouns, taking strong singular endings. Often, these adjectival nouns are preceded by the indefinite pronouns *etwas* ("something") and *nichts* ("nothing"). If a preposition precedes the words *etwas*, *nichts*, and *viel*, then it determines the case of the adjectival noun.

Listen and translate the following from German into English.

1. *Man trinkt viel Wein in Frankreich.*

....

2. *Man sagt so etwas nicht.*

....

3. *Haben Sie etwas Neues gehört?*

....

4. *Nein, ich habe nichts Neues gelesen.*

....

5. *Heute gab es nichts Interessantes in den Nachrichten.*

....

6. *Erzähl mir etwas Schönes.*

....

7. *Er gibt ihm etwas, was er sich leicht leisten kann.*

....

8. *Sag mir etwas, was ich noch nicht gehört habe.*

....

9. *Nichts, was er sagt, glaubt sie.*

....

10. *Dies ist etwas sehr Blödes.*

....

11. *Ich muss etwas Leckeres haben.*

....

Exercise 27

You inflect few indefinite pronouns in the genitive case, because their very meaning can be used only in the singular.

Examples are *jemand* ("someone, somebody"), *niemand* ("no one, nobody"), and *jedermann, jeder, jedem* ("everybody, everyone").

Translate the following sentences.

1. *Warum sprechen Sie mit jedem?*

....

2. *Das ist niemands Angelegenheit.*

....

3. *Das ist nicht jedermanns Sache.*

....

4. *Ich höre jemands Stimme.*

....

5. *Jemand spricht draußen.*

....

6. *Das Badetuch gehört niemand.*

....

7. *Nicht jeder kann nach Südamerika fahren.*

....

Exercise 28

You inflect pronouns derived from *ein*-words in all cases, and you use *beide* (an indefinite pronoun meaning "both") solely in the plural. Pay close attention to *einer* ("one"), *keiner* ("none, nobody"), and *jeder* ("each one"), which are inflected only in the singular.

Translate the following sentences.

1. *Fahren beide nach Bayern?*

....

2. *Die Eltern beider sind gestorben.*

....

3. *Jedes hat sein Gutes.*

....

4. *Keiner von beiden geht in die Disko.*

....

5. *Jeder hat seinen eigenen Geschmack.*

....

6. *Eines der Kinder hat einen Apfel.*

....

7. *Haben Sie mit einem gesprochen?*

....

8. *Einer von ihnen muss recht haben.*

....

9. *Sie sagten, keiner hatte es getan.*

....

10. *Ich kann jetzt mit keinem verhandeln.*

....

Exercise 29

Wenig ("little") and *viel* ("much") can be fully inflected, except in the singular, where they are frequently uninflected. Also, don't forget to pay close attention to *wenige* ("few, a few"), *viele* ("many"), and the plurals of *wenig* and *viel*, which you decline like the plural of the definite article.

Translate the following sentences.

1. *Die Meinung vieler ist nicht immer richtig.*

   ....

2. *Eine wahre Freundschaft ist nur mit wenigen möglich.*

   ....

3. *Ein weniges wird genügen.*

   ....

4. *Sie haben viel geleistet.*

   ....

5. *Sie kann aus wenig viel machen.*

   ....

6. *Er hat wenig erlebt.*

   ....

Exercise 30

You often use *all* ("everything") as a pronoun in the neuter singular and as an indefinite antecedent of a relative pronoun. Decline *alle* ("all of them") like a definite article in the plural.

Fill in the blanks using the following words: *Alles, alles, alle, allen*. Then translate the sentence in the longer blank.

1. *Es ist nicht* .... *Gold, was glänzt.*

   ....

2. *Nein, mit* .... *können wir nicht gehen.*

   ....

3. .... *gebe ich dir.*

   ....

4. *Grüße* .... *von mir.*

   ....

5. *Er ist mein Ein und* ....

   ....

6. *Das ist* .... *, was ich habe.*

   ....

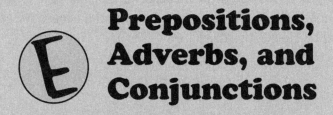

Part 4

Prepositions, Adverbs, and Conjunctions

This section deals with expanding simple sentence structures by providing more detail about prepositions, adverbs (the elements in a sentence that specify the time, manner, or place of an event), and conjunctions. Conjunctions are connectors between either two main clauses or a main and a subordinate clause.

Seven Important Prepositions Requiring the Accusative

Prepositions are followed by definite cases and can be categorized into four groups: prepositions followed by the accusative case, those followed by the dative case, those followed by either the dative or the accusative case, and those followed by the genitive case.

Exercise 1

TRACK 13

The seven prepositions *bis* ("to, till"), *durch* ("through"), *für* ("for"), *gegen* ("against"), *ohne* ("without"), *um* ("around, at"), and *wider* ("against") require the accusative.

Listen to and translate the following German sentences.

1. *Wir fahren bis Prag.*

   ....

2. *Warten Sie bis nächsten Dienstag!*

   ....

3. *Bis zum 2. habe ich kein Geld.*

   ....

4. *Sie geht durch den Park.*

   ....

5. *Dieses Geschenk ist für dich.*

   ....

6. *Was haben Sie gegen die Frau?*

   ....

7. *Sie gingen ohne die Schwester ins Kunstmuseum.*

....

8. *Sie fuhren mit dem Bus um die Stadt.*

....

9. *Wer nicht für mich ist, ist wider mich.*

....

Exercise 2

Fill in the blanks using the following words: customs, welcome, citizen, state, flood, funny, reason/use, surprise, cause.

1. *Flut* ....

2. *Grund* ....

3. *Ursache* ....

4. *Überraschung* ....

5. *lustig* ....

6. *Staat* ....

7. *Staatsbürger* ....

8. *willkommen* ....

9. *Gebräuche* ....

Eight Important Prepositions Requiring the Dative

There are eight important prepositions followed by the dative. The first three prepositions are *aus* ("out of, from"), *außer* ("except, beside"), and *bei* ("at, near, at the house of").

Exercise 3

Translate the following German sentences.

1. *Er ist beim Friseur.*

   ....

2. *Sie wohnt bei ihrem Onkel.*

   ....

3. *Oxford ist bei London.*

   ....

4. *Er ist bei der Arbeit.*

   ....

5. *Er war außer sich vor Ärger.*

   ....

6. *Alle waren da außer meinem Bruder.*

   ....

7. *Er trinkt aus einer Flasche.*

   ....

8. *Sie kommt aus dem Zimmer.*

   ....

Exercise 4

Circle the correct translation for each word.

1. *Geschäftsreise* (business trip, pleasure trip, educational trip)

2. *Vergnügungsreise* (educational trip, pleasure trip, business trip)

3. *Ankunft* (departure, arrival, closure)

4. *förmlich* (formal, form, front)

5. *Gast* (guest, gasoline, gulf)

6. *Frankreich* (French, France, Frankfurt)

7. *Wohnsitz* (residence, worship, window)

8. *tapfer* (coward, brave, scared)

9. *Nachkomme* (descendant, neighbor, village)

10. *Grundlage* (basis, garage, handbag)

Exercise 5

In all there are eight important dative prepositions. The remaining five prepositions are *mit* ("with"), *nach* ("after, to [a country or city]"), *seit* ("since," in statements of time), *von* ("from, of, by"), and *zu* ("to, to the house of").

Translate the following German sentences and phrases.

1. *Ich gehe zu meiner Tante.*

   ....

2. *Ein Gedicht von dem deutschen Dichter Goethe*

   ....

3. *Heute muss ich zum Arzt gehen.*

   ....

4. *Nach dem Essen geht er aus.*

....

5. *Kommen Sie mit mir nach Hause!*

....

6. *Wann fahren Sie nach Frankreich?*

....

7. *Seit dem 1. August habe ich sie nicht gesehen.*

....

8. *Dieses Geschenk ist von mir.*

....

9. *Die Hauptstadt von Amerika*

....

Nine Important Two-Way Prepositions

There are nine "two-way" prepositions, which require either the dative or accusative, depending on the context. You use the accusative case if there is motion to a place.

Take this sentence, for example: *Peter und Linda gehen in den Park*, which translates as "Peter and Linda are going into the park."

However, if these two are already in a park, then the sentence in German would be: *Peter und Linda sind in dem Park*. In this example the two-way proposition *in* is followed by the dative form *dem* because the two are already in a place and not going to a place.

Exercise 6

Translate the following German sentences.

1. *Wo gehen Sie spazieren? Ich gehe im Park spazieren.*

....

2. *Wo liegt der Kuli? Er liegt auf dem Schreibtisch.*

....

3. *Wo spielen die Mädchen? Sie spielen in dem Wohnzimmer.*

....

Exercise 7

Match the following German words with their English equivalents.

1. *Osten*   minute

2. *Baum*   window

3. *Wiese*   forest

4. *Fläche*   enormous

5. *Wald*   area/surface

6. *grün*   pretty/nice

7. *hübsch*   tree

8. *riesig*   green

9. *Fenster*   meadow

10. *Minute*   east

Exercise 8

The accusative is used if the context suggests motion to a place. Translate the following German sentences.

1. *Die Frau trägt das Bild in das Wohnzimmer.*

   ....

2. *Wohin gehen die Frauen? Die Frauen gehen in den Park.*

   ....

3. *Wohin legt er das Messer? Er legt es auf den Tisch.*

   ....

Exercise 9

Translate the following words.

1. *Bahnhof*   ....

2. *geradeaus*   ....

3. *Schaffner*   ....

4. *Nötige*   ....

5. *nochmals*   ....

6. *Schwarzwälder Kirschtorte*   ....

7. *jährlich*   ....

8. *Schwankung*   ....

9. *bedeutend*   ....

10. *Niederschlag*   ....

Exercise 10

TRACK 14

There are nine two-way prepositions. The first four prepositions are: *an* ("at, to, up to an object"), *auf* ("on, upon, on top of"), *hinter* ("behind, in back of"), and *in* ("in, into").

Listen and translate the following German sentences.

1. *Sie steht am Tor. Er geht an das Tor.*

....

2. *Die Pfanne steht auf dem Regal.*

....

3. *Sie stellt die Pfanne auf den Herd.*

....

4. *Er tanzt hinter mir.*

....

5. *Er stellt sich hinter mich.*

....

6. *Sie sind in dem Schwimmbad.*

....

7. *Sie kommen in das Gasthaus.*

....

Exercise 11

Fill in the blanks using the following words: amount, bathroom, bedroom, inhabitant, living room, kitchen, dining room, room, garage.

1. *Menge* ....

2. *Bewohner* ....

3. *Küche* ....

4. *Badezimmer* ....

5. *Garage* ....

6. *Zimmer* ....

7. *Esszimmer* ....

8. *Wohnzimmer* ....

9. *Schlafzimmer* ....

Exercise 12

There are nine two-way prepositions. The next three prepositions are *neben* ("beside, next to"), *über* ("over, above"), and *unter* ("under, among").

Translate the following sentences.

1. *Unter den Gästen sind viele Spanier.*

    ....

2. *Unter dem Schreibtisch steht der Papierkorb.*

    ....

3. *Er legt das Telegramm unter den Briefumschlag.*

    ....

4. *Er setzt sich neben seine Tante.*

    ....

5. *Er sitzt neben seiner Tante.*

    ....

6. *Ich hänge die Lampe über das Klavier.*

    ....

7. *Eine Lampe hängt über dem Klavier.*

    ....

8. *Ein Deutschlehrer wohnt über ihm.*

    ....

Exercise 13

Translate the following words.

1. *Küche*   ....

2. *Handtuch*   ....

3. *Seife*   ....

4. *Wohnung*   ....

5. *Schornstein* ....

6. *Papst*   ....

7. *Frühlingszeit* ....

8. *mittealterlich* ....

9. *heilig*   ....

10. *Gedicht*   ....

Exercise 14

There are nine two-way prepositions. The final two prepositions are *vor* ("before, in front of, ago") and *zwischen* ("between").
Translate the following German sentences.

1. *Er setzt sich zwischen meine Schwester und mich.*

....

2. *Er sitzt zwischen meiner Schwester und mir.*

....

3. *Vor einem Jahr ist er nach Italien gefahren.*

....

4. *Sie geht vor den Schrank.*

....

5. *Sie steht vor dem Schrank.*

....

Five Important Prepositions Requiring the Genitive

Anstatt ("instead of"), *statt* ("instead of"), *trotz* ("in spite of"), *während* ("during"), and *wegen* ("because of") are prepositions that require the genitive case.

Exercise 15

Translate the following sentences.

1. *Während des Tages arbeitet sie in einer Privatbank.*

....

2. *Ich konnte wegen meiner Kopfschmerzen nicht ausgehen.*

....

3. *Anstatt meines Vaters ging mein Bruder ins Konzert.*

....

4. *Trotz des schlechten Wetters blieb er nicht zu Hause.*

....

Exercise 16

Some of the following translations of German words into English are incorrect. Identify these and fix the mistake by translating the word properly.

1. *Dichtung* = furniture   ....

2. *siegreich* = victorious   ....

3. *Weltstadt* = closet   ....

4. *Leistung* = achievement   ....

5. *Macht* = piano   ....

6. *Klavier* = power   ....

7. *Dach* = balcony   ....

8. *Balkon* = roof   ....

9. *Schrank* = metropolis   ....

10. *Möbel* = poetry   ....

Exercise 17

The genitive case is not often used in modern German. In the future, the genitive case may actually be replaced by the dative case. Correspondingly, the prepositions commonly used with the genitive are used less and less frequently. Despite this, it is still valuable to know and practice the prepositions used in conjunction with the genitive case.

Translate the following less common genitive prepositions.

1. *unterhalb* ....

2. *oberhalb* ....

3. *diesseits* ....

4. *um . . . willen* ....

5. *außerhalb* ....

6. *jenseits* ....

7. *innerhalb* ....

Three Important Prepositions Requiring zu + Infinitive

You should use *anstatt* ("instead of"), *ohne* ("without"), and *um* ("in order to") with *zu* plus the infinitive. Make sure that *anstatt* and *ohne* come before the gerund, e.g., "going," "looking." When you state a definite intention, you have to use *um . . . zu* (in order to) with the infinitive.

Exercise 18

Translate the following German sentences.

1. *Wir besuchten unsere Großmutter, um ihren neuen Hund zu sehen.*

....

2. *Er verließ das Zimmer, ohne sich umzusehen.*

....

3. *Anstatt ins Theater zu gehen, besuchte er seinen Onkel.*

....

PART 4: PREPOSITIONS, ADVERBS, AND CONJUNCTIONS

Exercise 19

Translate the following words.

1. *Bild* ....

2. *Lampe* ....

3. *Spiegel* ....

4. *Laden* ....

5. *berühmt* ....

6. *Schwäche* ....

7. *Partei* ....

8. *Schutz* ....

9. *Hauptstadt* ....

10. *Sitz* ....

Common Contractions of Prepositions with Definite Articles

In the dative or accusative case, a few prepositions combine and contract with the definite article. Take a look at the following example: *in dem Park* contracts to *im Park*. Similarly, *Ich gehe zu dem Bäcker* contracts to become *Ich gehe zum Bäcker*. Here, the prepositions *in* and *zu* are contracted with the definite article.

Exercise 20

Translate the following contractions.
Question 1 has been answered for you.

1. *an + dem =*   *am*

2. *auf + das =*   ....

3. *in + das =*   ....

4. *in + dem =*   ....

5. *zu +der =*   ....

6. *von + dem =*   ....

7. *an + dem =*   ....

8. *an + das =*   ....

9. *zu + dem =*   ....

Adverbial Constructions

You can generally use any adjective as an adverb without changing the word.

Make sure, though, that you do not use *sehr* ("very"), *gern* ("like"), or *bald* ("soon") as adjectives, since they are pure adverbs. Nor can *gern* be used as a verb, since it only modifies a verb.

Gern haben (to like) frequently pertains to a person, but *gern* means "to like to" when it is with a verb other than *haben*, which then displays the tense, person, and number.

Exercise 21

TRACK 15

Listen to and translate the following German sentences and phrases.

1. *der schnelle Mann*

   ....

2. *Der Mann arbeitet schnell.*

   ....

3. *Sie geht sehr langsam.*

   ....

4. *Sie wird bald hier sein.*

   ....

5. *Er hat sie sehr gern.*

   ....

6. *Sie gehen gern tanzen.*

   ....

7. *Ich häkele gern.*

   ....

Exercise 22

Match the following words with their English translations.

1. *Abbildung*		United States
2. *Bau*		go shopping
3. *Brot*		Europe
4. *eng*		price
5. *Erklärung*		purchase
6. *Preis*		explanation
7. *Einkauf*		narrow/close
8. *Einkäufe machen*		bread
9. *Europa*		construction/building
10. *die Vereinigten Staaten*		figure/illustration

Exercise 23

When you attach the suffix -*weise* (from *die Weise*, "the manner, way") to an adjective, you derive independent adverbs (originally adverbial phrases) from adjectives. For example, *glücklicherweise* translates as "fortunately."

Be sure that you invert the word order when a sentence begins with an adverb or an adverbial phrase. This means that the verb comes before the noun.

Translate the following.

1. *Glücklicherweise kam er nicht so früh.*

   ....

2. *In der Nacht schläft er.*

   ....

3. *klugerweise*   ....

4. *gewohnterweise*   ....

5. *wunderbarerweise* ....

6. *unglücklicherweise* ....

Exercise 24

Translate the following words.

1. *Straße*   ....

2. *Allee*   ....

3. *Kirche*   ....

4. *Park*   ....

5. *Film* ....

6. *U-Bahnstation* ....

7. *Meinung* ....

8. *Seite* ....

9. *Strom* ....

10. *Werk* ....

Coordinating Conjuctions

There are two kinds of conjunctions. Coordinating conjunctions connect sentences, clauses, phrases, or words of equal rank. These coordinating conjunctions are "and," "but," and "or." Subordinating conjunctions (such as "when," "until," "although"), on the other hand, join dependent clauses with main clauses.

In German, the most frequently used coordinating conjunctions are

- *und* ("and")
- *enn* ("for")
- *oder* ("or")
- *entweder ... oder* ("either ... or")
- *sondern* ("but")
- *aber* ("but").

Keep in mind that the word order does not change after coordinating conjunctions. You must place the subject first and the verb second, following the normal word order in a sentence.

Exercise 25

Sondern is a more persuasive form of "but" that you are to translate as "but rather" or "on the contrary." Make the first part of the sentence negative, with the subject of the clause starting with sondern going back to the very same subject as the negative clause.

Translate the German into English.

1. *Entweder wir gehen sofort, oder wir werden zu spät kommen.*

   ....

2. *entweder . . . oder* ....

3. *Sie ist nicht dumm, sondern faul.*

   ....

4. *Sie fährt nicht nach Deutschland sondern macht eine Tour durch Spanien.*

   ....

5. *Er kaufte die Flugkarte nicht, denn er hatte nicht genug Geld.*

   ....

6. *Sie hat eine Karte für das Theater, aber sie kann nicht gehen.*

   ....

7. *aber* ....

8. *Wir müssen uns beeilen, oder wir werden den Autobus verpassen.*

   ....

9. *und* ....

10. *oder* ....

11. *denn* ....

12. *sondern* ....

Exercise 26

Translate the following words.

1. *Wien* ....

2. *Leiter* ....

3. *Abteilung* ....

4. *Gehalt* ....

5. *Kollege* ....

6. *Postamt* ....

7. *Krankenhaus* ....

8. *Polizist* ....

9. *Omnibus* ....

10. *Untergrundbahn* ....

Subordinating Conjunctions

Keep in mind that subordinating conjunctions demand dependent word order and are subordinate clauses.

Exercise 27

Translate the most common German subordinating conjunctions.

1. *wie*   ....

2. *bevor*   ....

3. *obgleich, obschon*   ....

4. *seitdem*   ....

5. *falls*   ....

6. *ob*   ....

7. *dass*   ....

8. *als*   ....

9. *als ob*   ....

10. *wenn auch*   ....

11. *ehe*   ....

12. *während*   ....

Exercise 28

Fill in the blanks using the following words: knife, order, silverware, bill/ check, tip, dessert, dishes, menu, fork, main course.

1. *Bestellung*   ....

2. *Rechnung*   ....

3. *Trinkgeld* ....

4. *Besteck* ....

5. *Geschirr* ....

6. *Speisekarte* ....

7. *Nachtisch* ....

8. *Hauptgericht* ....

9. *Gabel* ....

10. *Messer* ....

Exercise 29

Translate the following German conjunctions.

1. *wenn* ....

2. *nachdem* ....

3. *damit* ....

4. *je . . . desto* ....

5. *indem* ....

6. *wann* ....

7. *bis* ....

8. *wo* ....

9. *da* ....

10. *weil* ....

Exercise 30

Translate the following words.

1. *Boden* ....

2. *Bund* ....

3. *Reichsstadt* ....

4. *kaum* ....

5. *unabhängig* ....

6. *Verantwortung* ....

7. *Verhalten* ....

8. *Fernsehapparat* ....

9. *Radioapparat* ....

10. *Polizeiwache* ....

Dependent Clauses

Remember that you create a dependent clause when you join a clause with the main clause using a subordinating conjunction. You must utilize a special word order for the dependent clause. You are to place the verb proper at the end of the subordinate clause in simple tenses; the changed part of the infinitive or past participle precedes it in compound tenses.

Exercise 31

Translate the following sentences.

1. *Er tut es jetzt, weil er später keine Zeit mehr dazu hat.*

....

2. *Warten Sie nicht länger, da er heute nicht mehr kommen wird.*

....

3. *Er erkannte ihn, obwohl er ihn vierzig Jahre nicht gesehen hatte.*

....

4. *Ich weiß, dass er heute nicht zu Hause ist.*

....

Exercise 32

Circle the correct translation for each word.

1. *Restaurant* (rest area, café, restaurant)

2. *Rechnung* (bill, napkin, ring)

3. *Soße* (gravy/sauce, salt, ice cream)

4. *Kohl* (cabbage, pie, cake)

5. *Salat* (beans, corn, salad)

6. *Teller* (knife, plate, fork)

7. *Messer* (knife, plate, fork)

8. *Gabel* (knife, plate, fork)

9. *Suppenlöffel* (suppertime, dinner, soup spoon)

10. *Suppe* (supper, soup, soap)

The Three "Whens"

The conjunction *als* is commonly used to express that two events or circumstances happened at the same time in the past. You use *wann* if you are asking a question pertaining to time. In all other cases, use *wenn*.

Exercise 33

TRACK 16

Listen and translate the German sentences into English.

1. *Als ich ihn gestern traf, trug er einen silbernen Handschuh.*

....

2. *Als er in London war, ging er oft ins Theater.*

....

3. *Sie lebte in Österreich, als sie alt war.*

....

4. *Wann kommen Sie heute ins Sprachlabor?*

....

5. *Sagen Sie mir, wann Sie heute ins Geschäft kommen werden.*

....

6. *Ich weiß nicht, wann ich heute ins Büro kommen werde.*

....

7. *Wenn ich ihn sehe, werde ich es ihm sagen.*

....

8. *Wenn sie nach Hause kam, trank sie immer einen heißen Kakao.*

....

9. *Immer wenn er in Köln war, besuchte er den Dom.*

....

10. *Wenn ich in Wuppertal sein werde, werde ich Ihre Großmutter besuchen.*

....

Exercise 34

Translate the following words.

1. *Braten*   ....

2. *Gemüse*   ....

3. *Kartoffel*   ....

4. *Nachtisch*   ....

5. *Früchte*   ....

6. *Mittelalter*   ....

7. *Nacht*   ....

8. *tot*   ....

9. *fest*   ....

10. *Grieche*   ....

Inverted Word Connections

Adverbial conjunctions demand reversing the word order by placing the conjugated verb at the end of the sentence. *Damals* ("at that time"), *darum*, *deshalb*, *deswegen* ("therefore"), *teils . . . teils* ("partly . . . partly"), and *vielleicht* ("perhaps") are adverbial conjunctions.

Exercise 35

Translate the German into English.

1. *Vielleicht kommt er doch.*

   ....

2. *Teils kann sie nicht kommen, teils will sie nicht.*

   ....

3. *Ihre Schwägerin ist krank, deshalb kann sie nicht kommen.*

   ....

4. *Sie kommt heute selten, damals kam sie oft.*

   ....

Ⓔ Part 5
The Adjective

Nouns or verbs can be modified by adjectives. Take, for example, the sentence *Ich bin vorsichtig,* which translates to "I am careful." Here, "careful" is a predicate adjective with the verb *sein*. In another example, *Ich fahre vorsichtig,* which means "I drive carefully," the verb *fahren* is modified. It is now called an adverb, because this adjective modifies a verb. A third example, *Ich bin ein vorsichtiger Fahrer,* which translates to "I am a careful driver," illustrates an adjective that precedes a noun and has an ending.

Adjectives With and Without Endings

In *Ich bin ein vorsichtiger Fahrer*, the ending *-er* is attached to the base word "*vorsichtig.*" We call this adjective an attributive adjective, and we need to change the endings according to certain rules. The following adjectives are not declined:

- Adjectives following the verb *sein* as a predicate adjective
- Adjectives following *werden* ("to become, get")
- Adjectives that are derived from names of cities by attaching *-er*
- An adjective used as an adverb

Exercise 1

In the exercise below, pay close attention to the undeclined adjectives. Reconstruct the scrambled sentences and phrases and translate them.

1. *Mädchen gut das schreibt.* ....

....

2. *der liest gut Junge.* ....

....

3. *Eis das Münchener teuer ist.* ....

....

4. *der gut ist Film.* ....

....

5. *gut Buch ist das.* ....

....

6. *alt sie wird.* ....

....

7. *Berliner Theater ein* ....

....

8. *wird er alt.* ....

....

Exercise 2

Attributive adjectives precede the noun they modify. The endings of the attributive adjectives are determined by the gender, number, and case of the nouns they modify.

Pay close attention to the declined adjectives in the following German sentences and then translate.

1. *Die fleißige Studentin liest ein Buch.*

....

2. *Ein interessanter Artikel ist in der Zeitung.*

....

Unpreceded Adjectives

There are three basic groups of adjectives:

- Adjectives that are not preceded by *der*-words or *ein*-words, referred to as unpreceded adjectives.
- Adjectives preceded by *der*-words, such as *dieser, welcher,* etc.
- Adjectives preceded by *ein*-words, such as possessive adjectives, indefinite articles, and forms of *kein.*

The difference between the strong endings and the endings of unpreceded adjectives occurs in the genitive singular masculine and neuter.

The attributive adjective has the ending *-en* instead of *-es*. The phrases "*starken Kaffees*" and "*interessanten Buches*" illustrate this, as here the endings are *-en* instead of the *-es* the strong endings would require.

Exercise 3

Write the appropriate declined strong adjective form of *gut* for the masculine singular nouns (questions 1–4), the feminine singular nouns (questions 5–8), and the neuter singular nouns (questions 9–12).

Some of the answers have been provided.

1. Nom: *guter Vater*

2. Acc: .... *Vater*

3. Dat: .... *Vater*

4. Gen: .... *Vaters*

5. Acc: .... *Mutter*

6. Gen: .... *Mutter*

7. Dat: .... *Mutter*

8. Nom: *gute Mutter*

9. Dat: .... *Kind*

10. Acc: .... *Kind*

11. Nom: *gutes Kind*

12. Gen: .... *Kindes*

Exercise 4

Write the correct form of *gut* with the strong endings for the masculine plural (questions 1–4), the feminine plural (questions 5–8), and the neuter plural (questions 9–12). Fill in the blanks.

Some of the answers have been provided for you.

1. Acc: .... *Väter*

2. Dat: .... *Vätern*

3. Gen: .... *Väter*

4. Nom: *gute Väter*

5. Gen: *guter Mütter*

6. Acc: .... *Mütter*

7. Dat: .... *Müttern*

8. Nom: .... *Mütter*

9. Acc: .... *Kinder*

10. Dat: .... *Kindern*

11. Gen: .... *Kinder*

12. Nom: *gute Kinder*

Declining Weak Adjectives: Adjectives Preceded by der-words

The most common ending of the weak declension of the adjective is *-en*. Keep in mind that you have to attach the ending *-e* to the following five cases: the three nominative singulars and the accusative singulars of the feminine and the neuter cases. When one of the *der*-words has a distinct case ending coming before the adjective, you have to use the weak adjective declension.

Exercise 5

TRACK 17

Listen and translate the masculine singular nouns with weak adjectives (questions 1–4), the feminine singular (questions 5–8), and the neuter singular (questions 9–12).

Question 1 has been answered for you.

1. Nom: *der gute Vater*   the good father

2. Gen: *des guten Vaters*   ....

3. Dat: *dem guten Vater*   ....

4. Acc: *den guten Vater*   ....

5. Nom: *die gute Mutter*   ....

6. Gen: *der guten Mutter*   ....

7. Dat: *der guten Mutter*   ....

8. Acc: *die gute Mutter*   ....

9. Nom: *das gute Kind*   ....

10. Gen: *des guten Kindes*   ....

11. Dat: *dem guten Kind*   ....

12. Acc: *das gute Kind*   ....

Exercise 6

Fill in the blanks with the correct weak forms of *gut* for the masculine plural nouns (questions 1–4), the feminine plural (questions 5–8), and the neuter plural (questions 9–12).

1. Nom: *die* .... *Väter*

2. Gen: *der* .... *Väter*

3. Dat: *den* .... *Vätern*

4. Acc: *die* .... *Väter*

5. Dat: *den* .... *Müttern*

6. Acc: *die* .... *Mütter*

7. Nom: *die* .... *Mütter*

8. Gen: *der* .... *Mütter*

9. Dat.   *den* .... *Kindern*

10. Acc: *die* .... *Kinder*

11. Nom: *die* .... *Kinder*

12. Gen: *der* .... *Kinder*

Mixed Adjectives: Adjectives Preceded by ein-words

Ein-words are *ein, kein,* and the possessive adjectives. The *ein*-words have the same strong endings as the *der*-words except in three cases, where the *ein*-words have no ending at all. These cases are nominative masculine and neuter and accusative neuter. In these cases the adjective ending is a strong ending.

   If, however, the *ein*-words have an ending, then the adjective has the same weak ending as after a *der*-word.

Exercise 7

Write the correctly declined mixed adjective form of *gut* for the masculine singular (questions 1–4), the feminine singular (questions 5–8), and the neuter singular (questions 9–12).

Question 1 has been answered for you.

1. Nom: *ein guter Vater*

2. Dat: *einem* .... *Vater*

3. Gen: *eines* .... *Vaters*

4. Acc: *einen* .... *Vater*

5. Acc: *eine* .... *Mutter*

6. Dat. *einer* .... *Mutter*

7. Nom: *eine* .... *Mutter*

8. Gen: *einer* .... *Mutter*

9. Gen: *eines* .... *Kindes*

10. Acc: *ein* .... *Kind*

11. Nom: *ein* .... *Kind*

12. Dat: *einem* .... *Kind*

Exercise 8

Write the correct mixed adjective form of *gut* for the masculine plural (questions 1–4), the feminine plural (questions 5–8), and the neuter plural (questions 9–12).

Question 1 has been provided for you.

1. Nom: *keine guten Väter*

2. Dat: *keinen* .... *Vätern*

3. Gen: *keiner* .... *Väter*

4. Acc: *keine* .... *Väter*

5. Gen: *keiner* .... *Mütter*

6. Nom: *keine* .... *Mütter*

7. Acc: *keine* .... *Mütter*

8. Dat: *keinen* .... *Müttern*

9. Gen: *keiner* .... *Kinder*

10. Acc: *keine* .... *Kinder*

11. Dat: *keinen* .... *Kindern*

12. Nom: *keine* .... *Kinder*

Adjectives as Nouns

Germans frequently use adjectives as nouns. Keep in mind, though, that you still decline these words as you would decline an adjective.

Exercise 9

Decline the definite article for the masculine singular (questions 1–4), the feminine singular (questions 5–8), and the neuter singular nouns (questions 9–12), of *fremd* ("strange"), *alt* ("old"), and *klein* ("small"). Remember these adjectives are used as nouns.

Some answers have been provided.

1. Dat: .... *Fremden*

2. Acc: .... *Fremden*

3. Gen: .... *Fremden*

4. Nom: *der Fremde*

5. Dat: .... *Alten*

6. Acc: .... *Alte*

7. Gen: .... *Alten*

8. Nom: *die Alte*

9. Nom: *das Kleine*

10. Gen: .... *Kleinen*

11. Acc: .... *Kleine*

12. Dat: .... *Kleinen*

Exercise 10

Decline the masculine plural (questions 1–4), the feminine plural (questions 5–8), and neuter plural adjectives (questions 9–12) for *fremd*, *alt*, and *klein*. These adjectives are used as nouns.

Some answers have been provided.

1. Dat: ....*Fremden*

2. Gen: *der* ....

3. Nom: *die Fremden*

4. Acc: ....*Fremden*

5. Dat: ....*Alten*

6. Acc: ....*Alten*

7. Gen: ....*Alten*

8. Nom: *die Alten*

9. Gen: *der* ....

10. Dat: *den* ....

11. Acc: ....*Kleinen*

12. Nom: *die Kleinen*

Exercise 11

When an *ein*-word does not have an ending, the following adjective takes a strong ending. If you use any adjective as a noun after an inflected *ein*-word, then this adjective requires a weak ending like any simple adjective.

Translate the first two examples. For questions 3–5, find the correct *ein*-word and insert it on the line.

1. *die Große*   ....

2. *der Gute*   ....

3. Nom. Neuter: .... *Kleines*

4. Nom. Masculine: .... *Fremder*

5. Acc. Neuter: .... *Kleines*

Adjectives vs. Adverbs

The positive, comparative, and superlative are the three levels of comparison of the adjective and the adverb. When you attach the ending -er or -(e)st to the positive of the adjective, you compare the adjective. Observe, for example, the positive *klein* ("small"), the comparative *kleiner* ("smaller"), and the superlative *kleinst* ("smallest"). Although German has two superlatives, we will practice the more frequently used one with *am + -(e)sten*, as in the example *am ältesten*.

Exercise 12

Circle the German equivalents of the English words listed.

1. Superlative: poorest (*arm, am ärmsten, ärmer*)

2. Comparative: poorer (*arm, am ärmsten, ärmer*)

3. Positive: poor (*ärmer, arm, am ärmsten*)

4. Comparative: younger (*am jüngsten, jung, jünger*)

5. Positive: young (*jung, am jüngsten, jünger*)

6. Superlative: youngest (*jünger, am jüngsten, jung*)

7. Superlative: longest (*lang, länger, am längsten*)

8. Positive: long (*länger, lang, am längsten*)

9. Comparative: longer (*am längsten, länger, lang*)

Exercise 13

Questions 1–3 deal with *reich* ("rich"), and questions 4–6 deal with *langsam* ("slow").

Translate the following English words into German.

1. Superlative: richest ....

2. Comparative: richer ....

3. Positive: rich ....

4. Comparative: slower ....

5. Superlative: slowest ....

6. Positive: slow ....

Exercise 14

One-syllable adjectives require an umlaut on the stem vowel in the comparative and superlative. You also place an *e* in front of the ending *-st* to assist in pronouncing adjectives that end in a sibilant (*-s, -ss,* ß, or *-z*) or in *-d* or *-t.*

Questions 1–3 deal with *heiß* ("hot"), questions 4–6 deal with *kurz* ("short"), questions 7–9 deal with *mild* ("mild"), questions 10–12 deal with *alt* ("old"), and questions 13–15 deal with *weit* ("wide").

Translate the following English words into German.

1. Superlative: hottest ....

2. Comparative: hotter ....

3. Positive: hot ....

4. Comparative: shorter ....

5. Superlative: shortest ....

6. Positive: short   ....

7. Superlative: mildest   ....

8. Positive: mild   ....

9. Comparative: milder   ....

10. Positive: old   ....

11. Comparative: older   ....

12. Superlative: oldest   ....

13. Superlative: widest   ....

14. Comparative: wider   ....

15. Positive: wide   ....

Exercise 15

Note that in the comparative you take off the preceding *e* when adjectives end in -*el*, -*en*, or -*er*.

Questions 1–3 deal with *dunkel* ("dark"), questions 4–6 deal with *sauer* ("sour"), and questions 7–9 deal with *selten* ("rare").

Translate the following English words into German.

1. Superlative: darkest   ....

2. Comparative: darker   ....

3. Positive: dark   ....

4. Comparative: sourer   ....

5. Superlative: sourest   ....

6. Positive: sour   ....

7. Positive: rare   ....

8. Comparative: rarer   ....

9. Superlative: rarest   ....

Comparative Phrases

You must use *so . . . wie* to compare two equivalent states. An example of this is the sentence *Ich bin so groß wie du*, which means "I am as tall as you." The *so* + adjective + *wie* translates as "as + adjective + as."

Use the comparative with *als* (than) to state a comparison of adjectives of unequal states. Here are some examples:

Texas ist größer als Deutschland. "Texas is bigger than Germany."

München ist teurer als Berlin. "Munich is more expensive than Berlin."

Exercise 16

Match the German sentences with their English equivalents.

1. *Johann ist größer als mein Schwager.*

Johann is as tall as my father-in-law.

2. *Sie ist nicht so groß wie er.*

She is not as tall as he.

3. *Johann ist so groß wie mein Schwiegervater.*

Johann is taller than my brother-in-law.

Adjectives vs. Adverbs: Irregularity

A number of the most commonly used adjectives are irregular. Here are a few examples: *gut, besser, am besten*; *hoch, höher, am höchsten* ("high"); *viel, mehr, am meisten* ("many").

Exercise 17

Translate the following.

1. Superlative: most ....
2. Superlative: nearest ....
3. Comparative: more ....
4. Positive: near ....
5. Comparative: nearer ....
6. Positive: many, much ....
7. Superlative: greatest ....
8. Comparative: greater ....
9. Positive: great ....
10. Superlative: best ....
11. Positive: good ....
12. Comparative: better ....
13. Comparative: higher ....
14. Positive: high ....
15. Superlative: highest ....

Exercise 18

There are many variations and irregularities with adjectives. For example: *hoch* turns to *höher* in the comparative and *am höchsten* in the superlative.

Another example is *am größten*, which is an exception to the rule of placing an *e* in front of the superlative *-st* for every adjective ending in *-s* or another sibilant. When you use *viel* as an adjective, it is translated as "many." But when *viel* is used as an adverb, you translate it as "much."

Reconstruct the scrambled sentences and phrases below and then translate them.

1. *sie gegessen hat viel.* ....

....

2. *Kinder viele* ....

....

3. *Hotel hohe das* ....

....

4. *ist Hotel hoch das.* ....

....

Exercise 19

In the singular you translate *wenig* as "little," while in plural you translate it as "a few."

Translate the following.

1. *Was mache ich mit diesem wenigen Geld?*

....

2. *Wenige Kinder spielen heute auf dem Spielplatz.*

....

3. *Er hat wenig Zeit.*

....

4. *Sie hat wenig Geld.*

....

Exercise 20

You may use *früher* and *frühst* as both adjectives and adverbs, but *gern* is solely an adverb. When you use it with a verb, you substitute it for *mögen* (to like). You may also use the comparative and superlative of *gern* (*lieber* and *am liebsten*) as adjectives.

Translate the following German sentences and phrases.

1. *mein liebster Bruder*

....

2. *Sie singt gern.*

....

3. *Ich fahre früher.*

....

4. *Ich nehme den früheren Zug.*

....

The Comparative and the Superlative

Adjectives following *sein* and *werden* are uninflected in the comparative and superlative, and you use the structure of the superlative with *am* after *sein* and *werden*.

Exercise 21

Translate the following.

1. *Im Dezember sind die Tage am kürzesten.*

....

2. *Im Dezember werden die Tage am kürzesten.*

....

3. *Sie wird jeden Tag hübscher.*

....

4. *Der Sohn ist jünger, aber die Mutter ist weiser.*

....

Exercise 22

You decline comparative and superlative adjectives when they precede a noun.

Below, write the appropriate form of the adjective indicated. The answer to question 1 has been provided.

1. *der älterer Bruder* (*alt*, comparative)

2. *meine* .... *Schwestern* (*jung*, comparative)

3. *die* .... *Kinder* (*klein*, superlative)

4. *sein* .... *Kind* (*klein*, superlative)

5. *der* .... *Schwester* (*jung*, comparative)

6. *die* .... *Schwester* (*jung*, comparative)

7. *des* .... *Bruders* (*alt*, superlative)

8. *das* .... *Kind* (*klein*, superlative)

9. *die* .... *Brüder* (*alt*, superlative)

10. *ein* .... *Bruder* (*alt*, comparative)

11. *des* .... *Kindes* (*klein*, superlative)

Exercise 23

When the superlative comes before a noun, you use it as an adjective. For example, in the phrase *das interessanteste Buch*, which translates as "the most interesting book," the word *interessanteste* is the superlative and is used as an adjective with the appropriate ending.

When the superlative follows a verb, then you use *am* + the adjective, as in *Dieser Zug ist am schnellsten*, which means "This train is the fastest."

Translate the following into English.

1. *Johann schreibt besser.* ....

2. *Hans schreibt gut.* ....

3. *Aber Lois schreibt am besten.* ....

4. *mein bester Freund* ....

5. *Dieses Buch ist am besten.* ....

6. *das schönste Mädchen* ....

7. *Die Mutter ist am schönsten.* ....

8. *Dieses Buch ist das Beste.* ....

Cardinal Numbers

In German, you do not capitalize numbers except for *die Null* ("the zero"), *die Million* ("the million"), and *die Milliarde* ("the billion"). You also always write numbers as one word.

Exercise 24

TRACK 18

Listen and translate.

1. thirteen   ....

2. nineteen   ....

3. sixteen   ....

4. seventeen   ....

5. sixty   ....

6. seventy   ....

7. twenty   ....

8. thirty   ....

9. zero   ....

10. million   ....

11. billion   ....

12. one o'clock   ....

13. It is one o'clock.   ....

Exercise 25

Combine a cardinal number and *-mal* (from *das Mal,* "the time") to describe how many times something happens.

Match the German words with the correct English translations.

1. *zwanzigmal*   ten times

2. *dreimal*   three times

3. *zehnmal*   twenty times

4. *einmal*   thousand times

5. *tausendmal*   once

6. *viermal*   hundred times

7. *zweimal*   four times

8. *hundertmal*   twice

rcise 26

TRACK 19

Make ordinal numbers by attaching *-t* to the cardinal numbers from 1–19 and *-st* to numbers from 20 on. Decline ordinal numbers like adjectives and do not write them out if they are used in designating chapters or when stating dates or centuries. When you attach *-ens* to the stem of the ordinal number, you make numbers that are used adverbially. For example: *Erstens komme ich nicht, und zweitens…* translates as "first of all, I'm not coming, and secondly…"

Listen and translate the following German phrases and sentences.

1. *Der wievielte ist heute?*

   ....

2. *Heute ist der 3. (dritte) Juli.*

   ....

3. *Chicago, den 19. Oktober 1939. . .*

   ....

4. *Gestern war der 19. November.*

   ....

5. *Er ist am 12. August geboren.*

   ....

6. *Goethe wurde am 28. August 1749 geboren.*

   ....

7. *das 12. Kapitel*   ....

8. *erstens*   ....

9. *zweitens*   ....

10. *drittens*   ....

Exercise 27

Combine a cardinal number with *-tel* to construct most fractional numbers that are compounds, such as *ein Zehntel* ("one-tenth"). Do not decline these fractional numbers, but do decline *halb* ("half"), which is an adjective (declined as such) and is lowercase. Make sure that you take off the *-t* of *acht* before the ending *-tel*. Remember that the ending *-stel* is attached for numbers from *zwanzig* ("twenty") and above.

Translate the following.

1. *dreiviertel*   ....

2. *zweiachtel*   ....

3. *zweieinhalb*   ....

4. *Er gab ihr einen halben Euro.* ....

5. *ein Zwanzigstel* ....

6. *ein Achtel* ....

7. *anderthalb* ....

8. *dreieinhalb* ....

Exercise 28

When you do arithmetic, you spell *acht mal* ("eight times"), and *zwei mal* ("two times") in two words. The *mal* is colloquial for *multipliziert mit* ("multiplied by"), for example, *acht mal vier* (8 x 4). Otherwise, it is one word: *Ich klopfte zweimal an seine Tür.* ("I knocked twice on his door.")

Study the arithmetic below. Translated answers are provided in the answer key.

1. *Einmal die Woche geht sie ins Kino.*

    ....

2. *Ich bin schon dreimal bei ihr zu Hause gewesen.*

    ....

3. Divide: *Sechsundsechzig geteilt durch sechs ist elf*

    ....

4. Add: *Zwanzig und vierzehn ist vierunddreißig*

    ....

5. Multiply: *Acht mal neun ist zweiundsiebzig*

    ....

6. Subtract: *Zweiundfünfzig weniger sieben ist fünfundvierzig.*

    ....

Telling Time

In German, you state time in progression from one hour to the next and expect the succeeding hour when the time has advanced to the first quarter. For example, you say the equivalents of "it is a quarter past" and "it is half past," but Germans can also say *drei viertel elf* for 10:45. You also state time on the principle of a twenty-four hour day, like military time.

Exercise 29

TRACK 20

Listen and translate the following.

1. *um ein Uhr* ....

2. *um sechs Uhr* ....

3. *Es ist eins.* ....

4. *Es ist zwölf.* ....

5. *(ein) viertel fünf* ....

6. *halb fünf* ....

7. *drei viertel fünf* ....

8. *(ein) viertel nach fünf* ....

9. *(ein) viertel vor fünf* ....

10. *zehn Minuten nach zehn* ....

11. *fünf Minuten vor elf* ....

12. *(ein) viertel nach fünf* ....

13. *18.20 (achtzehn zwanzig)* ....

14. *24 (vierundzwanzig)* ....

Exercise 30

Use masculine and neuter nouns in the singular after numerals in statements of measure. After a singular number and in the plural after a plural number, you use a feminine noun of measure in the singular.

Translate the following.

1. *fünf Kilometer* ....

2. *zwei Kannen Kaffee* ....

3. *zwei Tassen Milch* ....

4. *eine Meile* ....

5. *eine Kanne Kaffee* ....

6. *vier Meter* ....

7. *zwei Liter Bier* ....

8. *ein Liter Bier* ....

9. *ein Glas Milch* ....

10. *ein Meter* ....

11. *eine Tasse Milch* ....

12. *zwei Gläser Milch* ....

Exercise 31

Use nouns describing monetary items (whether masculine, feminine, or neuter) in the singular (even with amounts of more than one).

Match the following German words with their correct English translations.

1. *ein Pfennig*   three pounds

2. *zehn Pfennig*   twenty euros

3. *drei Pfund*   one penny

4. *zwanzig Euro*   one pound

5. *ein Euro*   ten pennies

6. *ein Pfund*   one euro

Part 6

Verbs: Section A

This part considers the German verb, its regular and irregular conjugations, and its position in a sentence. Like English verbs, the ending of the verb in German changes with the subject. As a general rule and a reminder: The German verb consists of an infinitive, which is a stem and an -en ending—for example, *schreiben*, *lernen*, and *öffnen*. There are regular verbs, such as the three just mentioned, and then there are irregular verbs.

Three Irregular Verbs

Weak verbs and strong verbs are the two main groups of verbs. Practice on the various forms of the three irregular verbs *sein* ("to be"), *haben* ("to have"), and *werden* ("to become, get"), which are also used with compound tenses.

Exercise 1

Some of the English translations below are wrong. Find the mistakes and correct them.

1. *sie sind* = I am ....

2. *es ist* = you are ....

3. *Sie sind* = she is ....

4. *ihr seid* = it is ....

5. *er ist* = he is ....

6. *ich bin* = they are ....

7. *du bist* = you are ....

8. *sie ist* = we are ....

9. *wir sind* = you are ....

Exercise 2

Translate the present indicative of *haben*.

1. *ihr habt* ....
2. *Sie haben* ....
3. *wir haben* ....
4. *sie haben* ....
5. *ich habe* ....
6. *er hat* ....
7. *sie hat* ....
8. *du hast* ....
9. *es hat* ....

Exercise 3

Translate the present indicative of *werden*.

1. *sie werden* ....
2. *Sie werden* ....
3. *sie wird* ....
4. *ich werde* ....
5. *ihr werdet* ....
6. *er wird* ....
7. *es wird* ....
8. *du wirst* ....
9. *wir werden* ....

Exercise 4

Translate the past tense of *sein*.

1. *es war* ....
2. *sie waren* ....
3. *ihr wart* ....
4. *Sie waren* ....
5. *ich war* ....
6. *du warst* ....
7. *er war* ....
8. *sie war* ....
9. *wir waren* ....

Exercise 5

Translate the past tense of *haben*.

1. *es hatte* ....
2. *ihr hattet* ....
3. *wir hatten* ....
4. *sie hatten* ....
5. *Sie hatten* ....
6. *du hattest* ....
7. *ich hatte* ....
8. *sie hatte* ....
9. *er hatte* ....

Exercise 6

Match the examples of the past tense of *werden* with their translations.

1.	*sie wurden*	you (formal) became
2.	*sie wurde*	they became
3.	*wir wurden*	you (plural) became
4.	*ihr wurdet*	it became
5.	*Sie wurden*	I became
6.	*er wurde*	you (singular) became
7.	*du wurdest*	he became
8.	*ich wurde*	she became
9.	*es wurde*	we became

Exercise 7

Translate the present perfect tense of the following.

1. *er ist geworden* ....

2. *er hat gehabt* ....

3. *er ist gewesen* ....

4. *du hast gehabt* ....

5. *du bist geworden* ....

6. *ich bin geworden* ....

7. *du bist gewesen* ....

8. *ich habe gehabt* ....

9. *ich bin gewesen* ....

Exercise 8

Translate the following into English.

1. *wir sind geworden* ....
2. *sie haben gehabt* ....
3. *ihr habt gehabt* ....
4. *Sie sind geworden* ....
5. *sie sind geworden* ....
6. *wir sind gewesen* ....
7. *ihr seid gewesen* ....
8. *Sie haben gehabt* ....
9. *wir haben gehabt* ....
10. *ihr seid geworden* ....
11. *sie sind gewesen* ....
12. *Sie sind gewesen* ....

Exercise 9

Fill in the blanks with the correct translation of the past perfect tense.

1. *er war geworden* ....

(he had become, I had been, I had had)

2. *er war gewesen* ....

(he had had, I had been, he had been)

3. *er hatte gehabt* ....

(he had had, I had become, he had become)

4. *du warst geworden* ....

   (you had become, you had had, you had been)

5. *du hattest gehabt* ....

   (you had had, you have become, you had been)

6. *ich war geworden* ....

   (I had been, you had had, I had become)

7. *ich war gewesen* ....

   (I had been, he had had, I have become)

8. *du warst gewesen* ....

   (you had become, he had had, you had been)

9. *ich hatte gehabt* ....

   (I had become, I had had, I have had)

Exercise 10

Translate the following.

1. *wir waren gewesen* ....

2. *wir hatten gehabt* ....

3. *wir waren geworden* ....

4. *ihr wart gewesen* ....

5. *ihr hattet gehabt* ....

6. *ihr wart geworden* ....

7. *sie waren gewesen* ....

8. *sie hatten gehabt* ....

9. *sie waren geworden* ....

10. *Sie waren gewesen* ....

11. *Sie hatten gehabt* ....

12. *Sie waren geworden* ....

Exercise 11

Translate the future tense from German into English.

1. *er wird werden* ....

2. *er wird haben* ....

3. *du wirst werden* ....

4. *er wird sein* ....

5. *du wirst haben* ....

6. *du wirst sein* ....

7. *ich werde werden* ....

8. *ich werde haben* ....

9. *ich werde sein* ....

Exercise 12

Translate the future tense in the following German phrases into English.

1. *Sie werden haben* ....

2. *Sie werden sein* ....

3. *sie werden werden* ....

4. *sie werden sein* ....

5. *sie werden haben* ....

6. *Sie werden werden* ....

7. *wir werden sein* ....

8. *wir werden werden* ....

9. *ihr werdet haben* ....

10. *wir werden haben* ....

11. *ihr werdet werden* ....

12. *ihr werdet sein* ....

Exercise 13

Translate the future perfect tense.

1. *er wird geworden sein* ....

2. *du wirst gehabt haben* ....

3. *du wirst geworden sein* ....

4. *er wird gehabt haben* ....

5. *ich werde geworden sein* ....

6. *du wirst gewesen sein* ....

7. *ich werde gehabt haben* ....

8. *ich werde gewesen sein* ....

9. *er wird gewesen sein* ....

Exercise 14

TRACK 21

Listen and translate the future perfect tense.

1. *wir werden gewesen sein*

....

2. *wir werden gehabt haben*

....

3. *wir werden geworden sein*

....

4. *ihr werdet gewesen sein*

....

5. *ihr werdet gehabt haben*

....

6. *ihr werdet geworden sein*

....

7. *sie werden gewesen sein*

....

8. *sie werden gehabt haben*

....

9. *sie werden geworden sein*

....

10. *Sie werden gewesen sein*

....

11. *Sie werden gehabt haben*

....

12. *Sie werden geworden sein*

....

Two Major Groups of Verbs

Weak and strong conjugations are the two major verb groups. Practicing these verbs helps you to master the German language. Once you have a firm understanding of the difference between weak and strong verbs, then you can practice the past participles of these verbs.

Exercise 15

Match the following strong German verbs (questions 1–3) and the weak German verbs (questions 4–6) with the following words: sprang, to follow, followed, to spring, followed, sprung.

1. Past Participle: *gesprungen* ....

2. Infinitive: *springen* ....

3. Past: *sprang* ....

4. Past Participle: *gefolgt* ....

5. Infinitive: *folgen* ....

6. Past: *folgte* ....

Exercise 16

There is commonality between weak and strong verbs, but this commonality is limited to the present tense. You can find the stem of a strong or weak verb by removing the "en" from the infinitive. However, strong verbs have stem vowel changes such as from *a* to *ä* as in *ich fahre* and *er fährt*. The verbs also differ in the construction of past participles.

Place an *e* before the consonant ending in every weak and many of the strong verbs in the present tense if their infinitive stems end in -*t* or -*d*. Examples are *er wartet* ("he waits") *du wartest* ("you wait") *er wartete* ("he waited"), *er hat gewartet* ("he has waited"), *er findet* ("he finds"), *du findest* ("you find"), and *ihr findet* ("you find").

Don't forget to attach a *-t* in place of *-st* in the second person singular of the present tense if the infinitive stem of a weak or strong verb ends in *-s, -ss, -z,* or *-tz,* and ß attach the prefix *ge-* to the past participle to virtually every verb, along with *-t* to the participle ending of the weak verb and *-en* of the strong verb.

Translate the following.

1. *gegangen* ....

2. *er sitzt* ....

3. *gewohnt* ....

4. *du sitzt* ....

5. *er reist* ....

6. *ich sitze* ....

7. *du reist* ....

8. *sitzen* ....

9. *ich reise* ....

10. *reisen* ....

Direct Objects or No Direct Objects?

Remember that you are to conjugate weak or strong verbs in the compound past tenses with *haben* or *sein*. While a transitive verb demands a direct object in the accusative case, an intransitive verb cannot have a direct object.

Exercise 17

The following sentences with transitive verbs are scrambled. Reconstruct the complete sentences and then translate them.

1. *gehen die wir Kirche in.*

   ....

   ....

2. *antwortet ihr er.*

   ....

   ....

3. *er Lehrer erwartet seinen.*

   ....

   ....

4. *er liest Empfehlungsbrief den.*

   ....

   ....

Exercise 18

Certain verbs take the dative case and are therefore called dative verbs. The following exercise will provide you with some of these verbs.

Translate the following German verbs.

1. *helfen*   ....

2. *gehören*   ....

3. *begegnen* ....

4. *fehlen* ....

5. *gefallen* ....

6. *glauben* ....

7. *antworten* ....

8. *scheinen* ....

Exercise 19

Translate the following.

1. *dienen* ....

2. *geschehen* ....

3. *Er hilft seiner Schwiegermutter.*

....

4. *Er antwortet ihr nicht.*

....

5. *passen* ....

6. *folgen* ....

7. *Sie begegneten dem Dichter.*

....

8. *danken* ....

Rules for **Haben** *or* **Sein**

Make sure that you conjugate every reflexive verb, modal auxiliary verb, and transitive verb with *haben*.

Intransitive verbs, namely, verbs that do not take an accusative object, use the auxiliary *sein* instead of *haben*. Often these are verbs of motion, such as *gehen/ist gegangen*, meaning "to go" and *laufen/ist gelaufen*, meaning "to run." The following exercise focuses on "*haben*" and weak or strong verbs.

Exercise 20

TRACK 22

Listen to and translate the following German sentences.

1. *Sie hat eine Radtour gemacht.*

   ....

2. *Er hat den Roman gelesen.*

   ....

3. *Er hatte den Artikel gelesen.*

   ....

4. *Er wird die Nachricht gelesen haben.*

   ....

5. *Sie hat das Essen probieren können.*

   ....

6. *Sie hatte sich gesetzt.*

   ....

7. *Er hatte sich gekämmt.*

....

8. *Er hat ihr geantwortet.*

....

9. *Sie hat seiner Tochter geholfen.*

....

10. *Sie hatten den ganzen Tag gut gespielt.*

....

Exercise 21

Verbs conjugated with *sein* in the compound past tenses are intransitive verbs that manifest a modification from one place or condition to a different one, show motion toward, or indicate a change of status. *Ich bin nach Deutschland geflogen* ("I flew to Germany") is an example of this rule. The two intransitive verbs conjugated with *sein* that do not designate any modification are *sein* ("to be") itself and *bleiben* ("to remain").

Translate the following German sentences.

1. *Sie ist letzten Monat gestorben.*

....

2. *Ich war zu Hause geblieben.*

....

3. *Er war nicht gekommen.*

....

4. *Wir sind uns gestern auf der Straße begegnet.*

....

5. *Wo bist du gestern Abend gewesen?*

....

6. *Der Hund war seinem Herrn gefolgt.*

....

7. *Wir sind spät eingeschlafen.*

....

8. *Er ist auf die Post gegangen.*

....

Exercise 22

The present of *werden* and the infinitive of the chief verb create the future tense of weak or strong verbs. The infinitive of *haben* or *sein* and the past participle of the main verb (with the present tense of *werden*) create the future perfect.

Match the following German sentences with their English equivalents.

1. *Ich werde sie gesehen haben.*   I shall see her.

2. *Sie werden morgen gekommen sein.*   They will come tomorrow.

3. *Sie werden heute kommen.*   I shall have seen her.

4. *Ich werde sie sehen.*   They will have come tomorrow.

Tenses in Action

The present and future tenses (particularly in spoken German) are designated by the present indicative. In formal writing, you use the future tense for future events and use the present tense only to refer to something that occurs in the present tense. For example, *sie raucht* translates as "she smokes," "she is smoking" (progressive form), and "she does smoke" (emphatic form).

Exercise 23

Translate the following sentences that are in the present tense.

1. *Er wartet schon eine halbe Stunde auf ihn.*

   ....

2. *Ich kenne ihn zwei Jahre.*

   ....

3. *Wie lange kennen Sie Johann?*

   ....

4. *Wie lange wohnt sie schon hier?*

   ....

5. *Er ist seit zehn Jahre in den Vereinigten Staaten.*

   ....

6. *Wann fahren Sie in die Schweiz?*

   ....

7. *Ich fahre nächsten Herbst.*

   ....

8. *Sie gehen heute in die Stadt.*

   ....

Exercise 24

When you connect two or more events, you relate them to one another in time or sequence. For this reason, you conjugate them using the past tense.

Translate the following sentences.

1. *Sie arbeitete viele Stunden im Büro, bevor sie nach Hause kam.*

   ....

2. *Sie trank viel Milch.*

   ....

3. *Sie schrieb einen Scheck, als er ins Zimmer kam.*

   ....

4. *Er besuchte uns oft, bevor er nach Hamburg zog.*

   ....

5. *Gestern traf ich Herrn Zimmermann auf der Straße, und wir sprachen eine Weile mit einander.*

   ....

Exercise 25

When making a statement about one solitary unrelated action or truth in the past, you use the present perfect. Keep in mind that while you often use the present perfect to state related events in colloquial language, you do not do this in written German.

Translate the following sentences.

1. *Ich habe mir letzten Monat einen Mantel gekauft.*

   ....

2. *Rilke hat viele lyrische Gedichte geschrieben.*

   ....

Exercise 26

Use the past perfect tense to describe an action that happened in the past before another action in the past. Take, for example, the sentence *Ich hatte Michael besucht, bevor ich zu dir kam*, which means "I had visited Michael before I came to see you."

Translate the sentences below.

1. *Er hatte schon mit seinem Sohn gesprochen.*

   ....

2. *Sie hatte den Scheck schon geschrieben, als er ins Zimmer trat.*

   ....

Exercise 27

Using the future tenses with *wohl* ("probably") implies probability in the present.

Translate the following German sentences.

1. *Sie wird wohl verschlafen haben.*

   ....

2. *Die Telefonnummer wird wohl falsch sein.*

   ....

3. *Sie werden wohl wieder zu spät kommen.*

   ....

Two Kinds of Prefixes

There are two kinds of prefixes used with verbs: inseparable prefixes and separable prefixes. The separable ones are analogous to two-word verbs in English, such as "call up" or "find out." The inseparable prefixes modify the meaning of the verb they are attached to.

Exercise 28

There are seven prefixes that cannot be separated from a verb and used on their own. They are *zer-*, *ver-*, *ge-*, *miss-*, *be-*, *er-*, and *ent-* (or *emp-*). Translate and match the following.

1.	*zer-*	*zerreißen*	to mistreat
2.	*ver-*	*verstehen*	to break (completely)
3.	*zer-*	*zerbrechen*	to understand
4.	*ge-*	*gebrauchen*	to forgive
5.	*ver-*	*vergeben*	to use
6.	*miss-*	*misshandeln*	to tear
7.	*be-*	*besuchen*	to distrust
8.	*er-*	*erkennen*	to visit
9.	*be-*	*bekommen*	to receive, welcome
10.	*ge-*	*gefallen*	to originate
11.	*er-*	*erwarten*	to please
12.	*ent- (emp-)*	*entstehen*	to recognize
13.	*ent- (emp-)*	*empfangen*	to expect
14.	*miss-*	*misstrauen*	to receive, get

Exercise 29

Attaching a prefix to the verb modifies its meaning but the conjugation is still like the original verb. With inseparable prefixes, do no use the usual *ge-* prefix for the past participle.

Translate the following.

1. Future: *ihr werdet verstehen* ....

2. Future Perfect: *sie werden verstanden haben* ....

3. *erkannt* ....

4. *entstanden* ....

5. Past Perfect: *wir hatten verstanden* ....

6. *vergeben* ....

7. Present: *ich verstehe* ....

8. Present Perfect: *er hat verstanden* ....

9. Past: *du verstandest* ....

Exercise 30

In some tenses, the separable prefixes separate from their verbs. Divide the prefix from its verb and place it at the end of a sentence or phrase in simple tenses. For the verb *aufstehen* ("to get up") in the present tense, for example, the prefix *auf* has to be separated from the stem *stehen;* the conjugated form looks like *Ich stehe auf* ("I get up").

The prefix, however, cannot be the final part in a dependent clause. *Ich bin müde, weil ich so früh aufstehen muss*, which translates to "I am tired because I have to get up so early," is an example of this. Additionally, the prefix does not separate in compound tenses, for example: "*Ich bin aufgestanden.*" Note that you place the *ge-* of the past participle in the middle of the word after the prefix.

Translate the following German sentences.

1. Future: *Sie wird morgen um 5 Uhr aufstehen.*

    ....

2. *Ich weiß, dass sie jeden Tag um 5 Uhr aufstehen muss.*

    ....

3. Future Perfect: *Sie wird morgen um 5 Uhr aufgestanden sein.*

    ....

4. *Sie plante, morgen nicht um 5 Uhr aufzustehen.*

    ....

5. Imperative: *Stehe jeden Tag um 5 Uhr auf!*

    ....

6. Present: *Sie steht jeden Tag um 5 Uhr auf.*

    ....

7. Past: *Sie stand jeden Tag um 5 Uhr auf.*

    ....

Exercise 31

TRACK 23

When practicing mixed prefixes, you must remember that some of the prefixes are separable while others are sometimes inseparable. When you are using language in a literal sense, you separate the prefixes. When you use language in a figurative sense, you do not separate the prefix.

Listen and translate the following sentences that use three of the five most significant mixed prefixes. These three prefixes are *durch-*, *um-*, and *über-*.

1. *Ich durchsuchte meine Tasche.*

   ....

2. *Sie riss den Brief durch und warf ihn weg.*

   ....

3. *Der Zug fährt bis Hamburg durch.*

   ....

4. *Große Erleichterung durchfährt die Menge.*

   ....

5. *Sie umgeht meine Frage.*

   ....

6. *Dumme Gerüchte gehen um.*

   ....

7. *Dies umfasst die ganze Kaufhauskette.*

   ....

8. *Dies hatte die ganzen zehn Banken umfasst.*

   ....

9. *Sie setzt auf einer Fähre über.*

   ....

10. *Sie ist mit einem Kanu übergesetzt.*

    ....

11. *Sie übersetzt aus dem Isländischen.*

    ....

12. *Sie hat aus dem Norwegischen übersetzt.*

    ....

Exercise 32

The following sentences use the remaining two of the five most significant mixed prefixes: *unter-* and *wieder-*. Unscramble the sentence in each example and then write the translation.

1. *den Ball holt wieder der Mann.*

   ....

   ....

2. *sie Wort hat das wiederholt.*

   ....

   ....

3. *sie das wiederholt Wort.*

   ....

   ....

4. *hat er unterbrochen sie.*

   ....

   ....

5. *er im Hotel sie unter bringt.*

   ....

   ....

6. *unterstützen sie ihn.*

   ....

   ....

7. *er unterstützt sie hat.*

   ....

   ....

8. *der holt Mann den wieder Fernsehapparat.*

   ....

   ....

Verbal Nouns

You can use the gerund as a neuter noun. Nouns such as *die Schlafenden* ("the sleeping people") are called verbal nouns because the gerund and the infinitive are derived from verbs but used as nouns.

With a few exceptions, you derive nouns from the infinitive that are used solely in the singular. An exception is *das Leben* ("the life"), which has the plural *die Leben* ("the lives").

When you attach the suffix *-d* to the infinitive, you create the present participle. This form is used in German solely as an adverb or adjective (not in verb formation) and is inflected like any additional adjective. The past participle, along with its use in the conjugation of the perfect tenses and the passive mood, can be used as an adjective too.

Exercise 33

Translate the following.

1. *das gehende Kind* ....

2. *die geliebte Mutter* ....

3. *der singende Vogel* ....

4. *singend* ....

5. *ein gehendes Kind* ....

6. *das Kommen und Gehen* ....

7. *das Singen* ....

8. *das Tanzen* ....

9. *liebend* ....

10. *die liebende Mutter* ....

11. *gehend* ....

12. *das Sehen* ....

Exercise 34

When you use the past participle as an adjective, you use passive voice. In *die liebende Mutter*, the mother is the one doing the loving, but in *die geliebte Mutter*, the mother is the one being loved. Also note that with proper article and adjective endings, you can use present and past participles as nouns.

Circle the correct translation for each of the following.

1. *geschrieben* (lived, written, loved)

2. *das Geschriebene* (the lover, the written matter, the lighthouse)

3. *geliebt* (cooked, beloved, traveled)

4. *der Geliebte* (the chefs, the runner, the beloved one)

5. *die Liebenden* (beloved, joyous, the lovers)

6. *lieben* (to love, to write, to sign)

7. *reisen* (to speak, to travel, to sign)

8. *der Reisende* (the traveler, the writer, the signer)

Exercise 35

Use the infinitive with *zu* ("to") following specific prepositions such as *anstatt* ("instead of"), *um* ("in order to"), and *ohne* ("without") in infinitive phrases, and following *sein* with a passive translation.

Translate the following infinitive phrases.

1. *Das ist leicht zu lernen.*

   ....

2. *Hier ist viel zu sehen.*

   ....

3. *Sie kam in das Esszimmer, ohne mich zu sehen.*

....

4. *Sie geht zur Bank, um Geld zu wechseln.*

....

5. *Sie blieb bis 10 Uhr, anstatt nach Hause zu gehen.*

....

Commands

The imperative is a command or a suggestion. Whether the verb is part of the weak or the strong conjugation, you attach *-e, -(e)t,* or *-en + Sie* to the infinitive stem in order to create the imperative.

Exercise 36

Match the following German commands with their English translations.

1. *Gehen Sie!*   Go! (to a person addressed by *du*)

2. *Gehe!*   Go! (to a person addressed by *Sie*, singular and plural)

3. *Geht!*   Go! (to people addressed by *ihr*)

Exercise 37

TRACK 24

You must use *Sie* if you want to give a command or make a suggestion in the formal mode. You add an exclamation mark as the punctuation after the imperative. Place an *e* in front of the *-t* ending when the infinitive stem of a verb ends in *t, d, n,* or *m* when preceded by a consonant other than *l, m, n, r,* or *h.*

Listen to and translate the following.

1. *Warte!* ....

2. *Finde!* ....

3. *Öffne!* ....

4. *Gib!* ....

5. *Lies!* ....

6. *Nimm!* ....

7. *Sieh!* ....

8. *Trage!* ....

9. *Laufe!* ....

Exercise 38

When you use a reflexive verb in the imperative, state the reflexive pronoun as well.

There are a number of irregular imperative structures. For example, there is the imperative of *sein*: *Sei*! and *Seien Sie*!

Translate the following.

1. *sich anziehen*   ....

2. *Ziehe dich an*!   ....

3. *Stehe auf*!   ....

4. Accusative: *Freue dich*!   ....

5. *aufstehen*   ....

6. Dative: *Wasche dir die Hände*!   ....

Six Verbs on Their Own

A group of six verbs create an idiomatic conjugation of their own and are called the modal auxiliary verbs. These verbs require the infinitive of a full verb to finalize a sentence, except in special cases, discussed in Part 7. For example, "You must" is not a complete sentence in German, nor is "you may." These modal verbs require a verb such as "go" in "You must go" to make a complete sentence. However, these can be tricky because the modal auxiliaries are very idiomatic.

Exercise 39

Translate the six modal auxiliaries.

1. *müssen* ....
2. *wollen* ....
3. *können* ....
4. *mögen* ....
5. *dürfen* ....
6. *sollen* ....

Exercise 40

With the exception of *sollen*, the present tense requires a vowel change in the first, second, and third person singular of every modal auxiliary. The first and third person singular require no ending, but the forms of the plural acquire the endings of the present tense and are added on the infinitive stems.

Some of the examples below have mistakes. Find them and correct them.

1. *wollen* = should ....
2. *sollen* = want ....
3. *müssen* = must ....
4. *mögen* = to like ....
5. *können* = may ....
6. *dürfen* = can ....

Exercise 41

Translate the following German phrases.

1. *ihr könnt* ....
2. *wir können* ....
3. *sie können* ....
4. *du kannst* ....
5. *er kann* ....
6. *ich darf* ....
7. *er darf* ....
8. *du darfst* ....
9. *wir dürfen* ....
10. *ich kann* ....
11. *sie dürfen* ....
12. *ihr dürft* ....

Exercise 42

Translate the following.

1. *ihr müsst* ....
2. *sie müssen* ....

3. *du musst* ....

4. *wir müssen* ....

5. *er muss* ....

6. *ich mag* ....

7. *er mag* ....

8. *du magst* ....

9. *ihr mögt* ....

10. *wir mögen* ....

11. *ich muss* ....

12. *sie mögen* ....

Exercise 43

For every modal auxiliary, the conjugation in the present indicative of *können* ("can, to be able") functions as a standard. This means that the first person singular and the third person singular are the same conjugation: *ich **kann**, du kannst, er **kann**, sie **kann**, es **kann**, wir können, ihr könnt, sie können*. Translate *können* in the given tense and then match each phrase with its English equivalent.

1. Future Perfect Tense: *ich werde gekonnt haben*   I shall be able

2. Past Perfect Tense: *ich hatte gekonnt*   I could

3. Future Tense: *ich werde können*   I had been able

4. Past Tense: *ich konnte*   I have been able

5. Present Perfect Tense: *ich habe gekonnt*   I shall have been able

Exercise 44

The modals acquire the endings of the weak conjugation, except in the present tense, and in the second past participle when used with another verb.

Questions 1–4 deal with *dürfen*, 5–8 deal with *können*, and 9–12 deal with *müssen*. Answers 1, 5, and 9 have been provided for you.

Provide the principal parts (first person singular) of the modal auxiliary verbs in the tense indicated.

1. Infinitive: *dürfen* ("to be permitted")

2. Past: ....

3. Present: ....

4. Past Participles: ....

5. Infinitive: *können* ("to be able")

6. Past: ....

7. Present: ....

8. Past Participles: ....

9. Infinitive: *müssen* ("to have to")

10. Past Participles: ....

11. Present: ....

12. Past: ....

Exercise 45

A small change in the stem vowel occurs in the past tense. Also, you take out the umlaut of the infinitive in the past participle. Make sure that *sollen* and *wollen* retain their stem vowel. Modals acquire the weak endings except for the present tense and second past participle.

Questions 1–4 deal with *mögen,* questions 5–8 deal with *sollen*, and 9–12 deal with *wollen*. Answers 3, 7, and 10 have been provided for you.

Translate the principal parts of the modal auxiliary verbs.

1. Past: ....

2. Past Participles: ....

3. Infinitive: *mögen* ("to like")

4. Present: ....

5. Past: ....

6. Past Participles: ....

7. Infinitive: *sollen* ("shall")

8. Present: ....

9. Past Participles: ....

10. Infinitive: *wollen* ("to want, will")

11. Present: ....

12. Past: ....

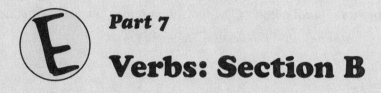

Part 7

Verbs: Section B

This section is the second part of our study of German verbs, and includes more in-depth explanation of the use of modals as well as the past tense of modal verbs, infinitives without *zu*, and the use of the subjunctive.

Is the Infinitive Required?

Modal verbs often require an infinitive to complete a sentence, but in colloquial German you often use the modal auxiliary with no accompanying infinitive if the meaning from the preceding statement or inquiry is obvious or if the meaning can be guessed. For example, a German might just answer the question: "May I come in?" with "Yes, you may." Instead of including the full verb "to come" (*kommen*), in this instance, it is understood.

Exercise 1

Translate the following German sentences.

1. *Er kann nicht mehr.*

   ....

2. *Sie muss fort.*

   ....

3. *Er wollte es.*

   ....

4. *Wollte er wirklich das Buch schreiben?*

   ....

5. *Nein, sie kann es nicht machen.*

   ....

6. *Sie kann Japanisch sprechen.*

   ....

7. *Kann sie die Arbeit machen?*

   ....

8. *Er will morgen kommen.*

   ....

Exercise 2

Circle the correct English equivalent for each of the following.

1. *dankbar*   (thank you, grateful, drink)

2. *Südamerika*   (Saudi Arabia, South America, Sweden)

3. *Büro*   (office, donkey, bunker)

4. *Geschäft*   (religion, business, legal letter)

5. *Kredit*   (credit, money, card)

6. *Geburtstag*   (baby food, Christmas, birthday)

7. *Unfall*   (accident, bridge, carpet)

8. *Mischung*   (mixture, liquid, Greek)

9. *Redner*   (reddish, speaker, melon)

10. *Salz*   (bronze, salt, iron)

Exercise 3

To form the past participle of the modal auxiliaries, create the regular past participle as a weak verb with the prefix *ge-* and the ending *-t*, using the stem of the infinitive of the verb. When using an infinitive with a modal auxiliary, do not use *zu*. Translate the following sentences.

1. *Sie hat Japanisch sprechen gelernt.*

   ....

2. *Er hat morgen nicht kommen wollen.*

   ....

3. *Er hat sie nicht gemocht.*

   ....

4. *Sie hatte es gekonnt.*

....

5. *Er hat es gewollt.*

....

6. *Sie hat es gekonnt.*

....

Exercise 4

TRACK 25

Listen to and translate the following.

1. *Gefühl* ....

2. *Wirklichkeit* ....

3. *Vergangenheit* ....

4. *Traum* ....

5. *sittlich* ....

6. *Inhaber* ....

7. *ledig* ....

8. *Nacken* ....

9. *Kamm* ....

10. *Schild* ....

Exercise 5

With modal verbs, in a main clause with simple tenses, you use the infinitive of the main verb at the end (as an example of this structure, see sentence 4 in the exercise below). With compound tenses, the modal infinitive is at the end preceded by the infinitive of the main verb (as an example of this structure, see sentence 3). Keep in mind that the modal is the last element in a sentence with compound tenses.

Translate the following German sentences.

1. *Ich weiß, dass sie heute nicht kommen können hat.*

....

2. *Sie hat es nicht gekonnt.*

....

3. *Sie hat nicht gehen können.*

....

4. *Sie kann nicht gehen.*

....

Exercise 6

Translate the following words.

1. *Ehefrau*   ....

2. *Friseur*   ....

3. *Lebensmittelgeschäft* ....

4. *Haarschnitt* ....

5. *Maniküre* ....

6. *geheimnisvoll* ....

7. *Gebiet* ....

8. *Entdeckung* ....

9. *Eisen* ....

10. *Kraft* ....

Exercise 7

Modals and many additional verbs that are part of the weak or the strong conjugation use the infinitive without *zu*. Don't forget that these additional verbs are either weak or strong.

Translate the German sentences below.

1. *Er lässt sich einen Anzug machen.*

    ....

2. *Haben Sie sich die Jacke in London machen lassen?*

    ....

3. *Ich habe ihn nie lachen hören.*

    ....

4. *lassen* ....

5. *Er geht einkaufen.* ....

6. *helfen* ....

7. *Er ist einkaufen gegangen.* ....

8. *gehen* ....

9. *hören* ....

10. *Sie hat ihr die Tasche tragen geholfen.*

....

11. *Sie half ihr den Koffer tragen.*

....

Exercise 8

Translate the following words.

1. *Ursprung* ....

2. *Vorlesung* ....

3. *Flug* ....

4. *Lebensbeschreibung* ....

5. *Angabe* ....

6. *Rasiermesser* ....

7. *Haar* ....

8. *Bürste* ....

9. *reizend* ....

10. *Träne* ....

Idiomatic Verbs in Action

You utilize *dürfte* (the subjunctive of *dürfen* for courtesy), and *können* ("to be able, can") is translated as "an ability to perform or do something" or to "know how."

    Mögen means "to like," and if you put the adverb *gern* after *möchte* (the subjunctive of *mögen*), it means "should like to."

Exercise 9

Translate the following sentences.

1. *Er möchte gern ins Kino gehen.*

....

2. *Das mag falsch sein.*

....

3. *Er hat sie gern.*

....

4. *Er mag sie nicht.*

....

5. *Sie möchten gern nach China fahren.*

   ....

6. *Darf ich eine Frage stellen?*

   ....

7. *Sie kann nicht zum Konzert gehen.*

   ....

8. *Können Sie tanzen?*

   ....

9. *Sie konnte nicht singen.*

   ....

10. *Darf sie die Tür öffnen?*

   ....

Exercise 10

Match the following words.

1.	*Ausländer*	tourism
2.	*Polizei*	pure/clean
3.	*Papier*	earth
4.	*Feder*	calendar
5.	*Kalender*	health
6.	*Seite*	page
7.	*Erde*	pen
8.	*Gesundheit*	paper
9.	*rein*	police
10.	*Fremdenverkehr*	foreigner

Exercise 11

TRACK 26

Practice writing the meaning of *müssen* ("to have to, must"), *sollen* ("to be expected, shall"), and *wollen* ("to intend to" and "to claim to"). In the past subjunctive, you are to translate *sollen* as "ought to."

Listen and translate into English.

1. *Jedes Kind muss mit fünf Jahren zur Vorschule gehen.*

   ....

2. *Ich musste gestern nähen.*

   ....

3. *Du musst das nicht glauben.*

   ....

4. *Du sollst Vater und Mutter besuchen.*

   ....

5. *Wir sollten ihn heute im Kino treffen.*

   ....

6. *Sie soll ein deutsches Gericht kochen.*

   ....

7. *Sie soll sehr intelligent sein.*

   ....

8. *Sie sollen in Europa sein.*

   ....

9. *Sie will Polnisch lernen.*

   ....

10. *Er wollte sie nicht wiedersehen.*

   ....

11. *Ich wollte es tun, aber ich hatte keine Zeit.*

....

12. *Er wollte gerade fortgehen, als sie kam.*

....

13. *Sie will gebildet sein.*

....

14. *Sie wollte es gewesen sein.*

....

Exercise 12

Translate the following words.

1. *Suche*   ....

2. *Flugzeug*   ....

3. *Übersetzung*   ....

4. *Gesetzgebung*   ....

5. *Soldat*   ....

6. *Briefmarke*   ....

7. *Briefumschlag*   ....

8. *Ausverkauf*   ....

9. *Bluse*   ....

10. *Rock*   ....

Wissen ("to know") and Lassen ("to let")

Remember that *wissen*, meaning "to know (a fact)", has a conjugation like the modals, but is not, in fact, a modal auxiliary verb.

Exercise 13

Translate the following.

1. Past: *sie wussten* ....

2. Present: *ihr wisst* ....

3. Present: *wir wissen* ....

4. Past: *ihr wusstet* ....

5. Present: *sie wissen* ....

6. Past: *wir wussten* ....

7. Present: *du weißt* ....

8. Past: *ich wusste* ....

9. Present: *er weiß* ....

10. Past: *du wusstest* ....

11. Present: *ich weiß* ....

12. Past: *er wusste* ....

Exercise 14

Match the following German words with their English counterparts.

1. *Pullover*   black

2. *Regenschirm*   neighbor

3. *rosa*   immigrant

4. *blau*   gray

5. *weiß*   knowledge

6. *grau*   sweater

7. *Erkenntnis*   blue

8. *Nachbar*   white

9. *Einwanderer*   umbrella

10. *schwarz*   pink

Exercise 15

Wissen conjugates as a weak verb. Translate *wissen* as "to know (a fact)," *können* as "to know, to be able," and *kennen* as "to know, be acquainted with."

Translate the following sentences.

1. *Ich kenne Bern.*

....

2. *Kennen Sie Herrn Jacobs?*

....

3. *Können Sie den Stuhl heben?*

....

4. *Ich kann Chinesisch sprechen.*

....

5. *Er kann nicht kochen.*

....

6. *Sie weiß, wann die Feier beginnt.*

....

7. *Sie weiß, dass du Katrin heißt.*

....

Exercise 16

Translate the following words.

1. *Angestellter*   ....

2. *Zelle*   ....

3. *Stimme*   ....

4. *Kreuz*   ....

5. *Erfolg*   ....

6. *Wachstum*   ....

7. *vollkommen*   ....

8. *Spiegelei*   ....

9. *Loch*   ....

10. *teilnahmsvoll*   ....

Exercise 17

TRACK 27

Lassen is translated as "to be," "to leave," or "to have something done or to cause something to be done." Translate *lassen* with a reflexive infinitive as "to have something done."

Listen and translate into English.

1. *Sie lässt mich nicht fernsehen.*

....

2. *Lass mich allein!*

....

3. *Sie ließ einen Arzt kommen.*

....

4. *Ich lasse mir ein Kleid machen.*

....

5. *Sie ließ sich eine Flasche Wasser bringen.*

....

6. *Das lässt sich leicht denken.*

....

Exercise 18

Circle the correct translation for each word.

1. *volkstümlich*   (folksy, car, folk song)

2. *Schloß*   (castle, sore, farm)

3. *Grenze*   (border/boundary, green, grass)

4. *Schlacht*   (shoe, battle, school)

5. *Bekannte*   (friend, enemy, acquaintance)

6. *Zusammensetzung*   (composition, zoo, wagon)

7. *trotzdem*   (seldom, sometimes, nevertheless)

8. *durchschnittlich*   (excellent, poor, average)

9. *tief*   (deep/low, high, width)

10. *Lauf*   (sample, course, letter)

Exercise 19

Translate the following words.

1. *Koch*   ....

2. *geheim*   ....

3. *Stahl*   ....

4. *stark*   ....

5. *Teil*   ....

6. *Breite*   ....

7. *Druck*   ....

8. *Breitengrad*   ....

9. *Siedepunkt*   ....

10. *Beobachtung*   ....

Construction of Passive Verbs

Use the different forms of the auxiliary verb *werden* ("to become") for the passive voice. Make sure that you put the past participle, *worden*, at the end of the sentence. You create *worden* by taking off the *ge-* of the regular form of the past participle, *geworden*. Use this form in the present perfect, past perfect, and future perfect tenses of the passive.

Exercise 20

In German, you often use verbs with the indefinite pronoun *man* ("one, they, people") in the active voice to convey a passive meaning. Take the sentence *Man singt gern in Deutschland*, for example. This translates to "One likes to sing in Germany." If you want to turn this active sentence into passive, then the impersonal pronoun *es* (expressed or understood) becomes the subject of the sentence in the passive. The same sentence above becomes now in the passive voice "*Es wird viel in Deutschland gesungen*". If the sentence possesses an adverbial phrase or adverb, you begin the passive sentence with the adverb. Do not use the subject *es* ("it"), with such a construction because it is understood in the sentence.

Translate the following sentences.

1. *Gestern wurde viel gelacht und gesungen.*

   ....

2. *Hier wird Finnisch gesprochen.*

   ....

3. *Der Titel des Buches ist von dem Autoren erwähnt worden.*

   ....

4. *Kann man im Rhein schwimmen?*

   ....

5. *Man sollte immer seine Meinung sagen.*

....

6. *Den alten Leuten wird von den Kindern geholfen.*

....

7. *Die Kinder helfen den alten Leuten.*

....

8. *Du warst nicht eingeladen worden.*

....

9. *Der Autor erwähnt den Titel des Buches.*

....

10. *Man hat dich nicht eingeladen.*

....

Exercise 21

Translate the following words.

1. *Greis* ....

2. *Lebensdauer* ....

3. *neugeboren* ....

4. *Seuche* ....

5. *Steigerung* ....

6. *Prüfung* ....

7. *Quelle* ....

8. *Regel* ....

9. *Stück* ....

10. *Zuwachs* ....

Exercise 22

TRACK 28

The tenses of *werden* state the true passive, which designates an action occurring at distinct times.

There are many substitutes for the passive. Possible substitutes are: *man* ("one, people, they") as an indefinite subject of a sentence, the reflexive verb *lassen* ("to let"), translated as "can," and *sein* ("to be") with an infinitive and *zu*.

A false passive is conjugated with *sein* that depicts a state or condition of the subject. This is not an action.

Listen and translate into English.

1. *Die Kirche wird gebaut.*

   ....

2. *Die Mauer ist aus Stein gebaut.*

   ....

3. *Die Brücke wurde im Jahre 1890 gebaut.*

   ....

4. *Das Restaurant ist geöffnet.*

   ....

5. *Die neue Bücherei wird im Sommer geöffnet.*

   ....

6. *Man kann nie wissen.*

   ....

7. *Man tut das nicht.*

   ....

8. *Es freut mich sehr.*

   ....

9. *Das versteht sich.*

   ....

10. *Sie interessierte sich für ihn.*

   ....

11. *Das lässt sich leicht ändern.*

....

12. *Das ist zu erwarten.*

....

Exercise 23

Circle the correct translation for the following words.

1. *Erzieher*   (educator, mayor, student)

2. *Betragen*   (baker, balloon, behavior)

3. *Schlange*   (snake/serpent, lamb, lizard)

4. *Frau*   (woman, turtle, wind)

5. *Muskel*   (muscle, musket, music)

6. *Leser*   (reader, speaker, light)

7. *Wirtschaft*   (science, politics, economy)

8. *Wunder*   (thunder, wonder/miracle, movie star)

9. *Schriftsteller*   (star, writer/author, movie star)

10. *Seele*   (soul, steel, seal)

Possibility and Uncertainty

The subjunctive mood designates that which is possible, uncertain, desirable, doubtful, or contrary to fact, and is also used with indirect statements. In the subjunctive mood, the personal endings are alike for every tense for every verb. In order for you to state present tense, there are two forms of the verb in the subjunctive mood. Subjunctive I is constructed on the infinitive stem.

Exercise 24

Fill in the blanks with the present tense of subjunctive I for the verb *machen*.

1. *sie* ....
2. *wir* ....
3. *ihr* ....
4. *ich* ....
5. *du* ....
6. *er* ....

Exercise 25

Translate the following words.

1. *sichtbar* ....
2. *Behauptung/Bestimmung* ....
3. *Schicksal* ....
4. *Petrus* ....
5. *Straßenbahn* ....
6. *Friede* ....
7. *Sturm* ....
8. *zeitlos* ....
9. *schöpferisch* ....
10. *leidenschaftlich* ....

Exercise 26

Question 1 has been answered.

Fill in the blanks with the present tense of subjunctive I for the verb *sein*.

1. *sein*   to be

2. *sie*   ....

3. *ihr*   ....

4. *ich*   ....

5. *wir*   ....

6. *er*   ....

7. *du*   ....

Exercise 27

Translate the following words.

1. *Räuber*   ....

2. *Leiden*   ....

3. *Abschnitt*   ....

4. *Beobachtung*   ....

5. *Fürst*   ....

6. *Spiel*   ....

7. *Zukunft* ....

8. *königlich* ....

9. *Schach* ....

10. *Wurzel* ....

Exercise 28

Subjunctive II is constructed on the past tense stem. Fill in the blanks with the present tense of subjunctive II for the verb *machen*. The first question has been answered. Also, translate sentences 2 and 4.

1. *ich   machte*

2. *Wenn sie nur hier wäre!*

   ....

3. *sie* ....

4. *Sie sieht aus, als ob sie müde sei.*

   ....

5. *du* ....

6. *wir* ....

7. *ihr* ....

8. *er* ....

Exercise 29

Translate the following words.

1. *Kühlung* ....

2. *Stuhl* ....

3. *gebildet* ....

4. *Mauer* ....

5. *Vorurteil* ....

6. *Opfer* ....

7. *Bürger* ....

8. *Grad* ....

9. *Titel* ....

10. *Feuchtigkeit* ....

Exercise 30

With the subjunctive mood, you only state past action in the compound tenses. When the auxiliary verb in the present perfect, past perfect, future, or future perfect tense is modified to the subjunctive form, you create compound tenses.

Translate the following according to the given tense. Some of the answers have been provided.

1. Future Perfect: .... he will have been made

2. Future Perfect: .... you will have been made

3. Future Perfect: *ich werde gemacht haben*

4. Future: .... he will make

5. Future: .... you will make

6. Future: *ich werde machen*

7. Past Perfect: .... he had made

8. Past Perfect: .... you had made

9. Past Perfect: *ich hätte gemacht*

10. Present Perfect: .... he had made

11. Present Perfect: .... you had made

12. Present Perfect: *ich habe gemacht*

Exercise 31

Translate the following words and write a sentence in German using each word. The first line is for the translation and the second line is for your sentence.

1. *gelb*   ....

....

2. *Ratte*   ....

....

3. *Leiter*   ....

....

4. *Übung* ....

....

5. *Liebe* ....

....

6. *Gespräch* ....

....

7. *Blatt* ....

....

8. *Befehl* ....

....

9. *Schweiz* ....

....

10. *Persönlichkeit* ....

....

Possibility in Action

You use the subjunctive in indirect discourse when you are repeating or reporting what someone stated, wrote, or told. Another instance in which you would use the subjunctive is for wishful thinking. For example: *Ich würde mir ein Haus kaufen, wenn ich Geld hätte—aber ich habe keins*, which means "I would buy a house if I had money—but I don't have any."

In indirect discourse in spoken German, on the other hand, you use the indicative mood instead of the subjunctive mood.

Exercise 32

Translate the following.

1. *Er tat, als ob er sie nie gesehen hätte.*

....

2. *Sie sah aus, als ob sie die ganze Nacht nicht geschlafen hätte.*

....

3. *Hätte er es mir doch gesagt!*

....

4. *Hätte er nur Zeit!*

....

5. *Er sieht aus, als ob er müde wäre.*

....

6. *Wenn sie nur nicht so müde gewesen wäre!*

....

7. *Möge er glücklich sein!*

....

8. *Sie schrieb, dass sie ihn letzten Monat gesehen hätte.*

....

9. *Sie ruhe in Frieden!*

....

10. *Wäre sie doch zu Hause!*

....

11. *Sie sagt, dass sie morgen keine Zeit habe* (or *hätte*).

....

12. *Wenn sie es nur nicht sähe!*

....

Exercise 33

Translate the following words.

1. *Bahnbrecher* ....
2. *Arznei* ....
3. *giftig* ....
4. *begraben* ....
5. *Chirurgie* ....
6. *Irrsinn* ....
7. *hervorragend* ....
8. *Gestalt* ....
9. *Stern* ....
10. *Vertrag* ....

Exercise 34

In extremely literary expressions, such as *Möge sie in Frieden ruhen* ("may she rest in peace"), you use the subjunctive mood. The subjunctive is also used in indirect discourse, in statements of doubt or possibility, in courteous statements founded on modal auxiliaries, and in commands.

Translate the following sentences.

1. *Man sollte so etwas nicht sagen.*

....

2. *Nehmen sie den Zug!*

....

3. *Lassen wir uns jetzt gehen!*

....

4. *Ich möchte Sie gern begleiten.*

....

5. *Das wäre ein Irrtum.*

....

6. *Es konnte falsch sein.*

....

7. *Es ließe sich machen.*

....

8. *Würden sie kommen mögen?*

....

9. *Wäre es Ihnen recht?*

....

10. *Dürfte ich um den Pfeffer bitten?*

....

Exercise 35

Translate the following words.

1. *Strahl* ....

2. *Konkurrenzkampf* ....

3. *Hypnose* ....

4. *klug* ....

5. *Tod* ....

6. *Erbschaft* ....

7. *Schüler* ....

8. *Befehl* ....

9. *Wiedervereinigung* ....

10. *Maus* ....

Two Conditional Tenses

The conditional has two tenses: the present conditional and the past conditional. You use the past subjunctive of *werden* ("to become") with the infinitive of the verb to create the present tense of the conditional. The present conditional resembles the future, utilizing *würden* in place of *werden*.

Exercise 36

Match the following sentences.

1. *ich würde antworten*   I would answer

2. *ich würde haben*   he would go

3. *ich würde sein*   she would write

4. *sie würde schreiben*   I would have

5. *er würde gehen*   I would be

Exercise 37

Translate the following words.

1. *Gewicht* ....
2. *Welle* ....
3. *Mond* ....
4. *Inhalt* ....
5. *Biene* ....
6. *Tanz* ....
7. *Pilz* ....
8. *Vorfall* ....
9. *Abwehr* ....
10. *Ausrüstung* ....

Exercise 38

Use the past subjunctive of *werden* with the past participle of the verb and the infinitive *haben* or *sein* in order to create the past conditional. Notice that the past conditional looks like the future perfect tense, utilizing *würden* instead of *werden*.

Translate the following.

1. *ich würde geantwortet haben*

....

2. *ich würde gewesen sein*

....

3. *ich würde gehabt haben*

....

Exercise 39

Translate the following words.

1. *Vererbungslehre* ....
2. *Pulver* ....
3. *Huhn* ....
4. *Zaun* ....
5. *Sünde* ....
6. *neuzeitlich* ....
7. *Skizze* ....
8. *wahrscheinlich* ....
9. *Enkelkind* ....
10. *Tatkraft* ....

Exercise 40

The conditional expresses present and past time and is used with propositions that are not actual, but rather theoretical, and in contrary-to-fact or -reality statements, such as in the sentence *Wäre er doch nur pünktlich!* which means "If he would only be punctual!"

In stating the conclusion in a contrary-to-fact statement, the subjunctive is desired in the conclusion with strong verbs. You generally use the conditional in the conclusion (particularly in the present tense) with weak verbs. Do not use the conditional in the *wenn,* or "if" clause.

Translate the following.

1. *Wenn sie Geld hätte, würde sie eine Jacht kaufen (. . . kaufte sie eine Jacht).*

   ....

2. *Sie hätte gestern einen Spaziergang gemacht (or . . . Sie würde gestern einen Spaziergang gemacht haben), wenn sie Zeit gehabt hätte.*

   ....

3. *Wäre ich sie gewesen, hätte ich das nicht getan (or . . . würde ich das nicht getan haben).*

   ....

4. *Wäre ich Sie, täte ich das nicht.*

   ....

5. *Wenn sie Geld gehabt hätte, würde sie sich letztes Jahr ein Haus gekauft haben (or . . . hätte sie sich letztes Jahr ein Haus gekauft).*

   ....

6. *Sie würde einen Spaziergang machen, wenn sie Zeit hätte.*

   ....

7. *Wenn er Geld hätte, würde er ein Haus kaufen.*

   ....

Exercise 41

Translate the following words.

1. *Grund* ....

2. *Freund* ....

3. *wahr* ....

4. *Mitglied* ....

5. *Gesundheit* ....

6. *Bücherei* ....

7. *Wörterbuch* ....

8. *himmlisch* ....

9. *Ofen* ....

10. *Brand* ....

Exercise 42

Let's now examine the impersonal construction of verbs. Remember that in statements pertaining to phenomena of nature, you use a good number of verbs with *es* (it) as an indefinite subject.

Translate the following.

1 *Diese Ereignisse geschahen vor einem Monat.*

....

2. *Es geschieht dir recht.*

....

3. *es donnert* ....

4. *Die Experimente gelangen ihr gut.*

   ....

5. *es schneit* ....

6. *es blitzt* ....

7. *es regnet* ....

8. *Es gelingt ihr nicht, weiterzukommen.*

   ....

Exercise 43

Match the following words by choosing the correct translation.

1.	*Fahrrad*	treasure
2.	*Holz*	raisin
3.	*Gelächter*	place
4.	*Kette*	mission
5.	*Geheimnis*	bicycle
6.	*Zucker*	laughter
7.	*Schatz*	wood
8.	*Rosine*	chain
9.	*Einsatz*	sugar
10.	*Ort*	secret

Exercise 44

Use other verbs impersonally in idiomatic statements such as "it seems," "it looks," etc., and in a number of statements pertaining to emotional or physical conditions. When the *es* is substituted by a concrete thing (which is then the subject of the sentence), you generally designate the reaction or emotion by the dative case ("Cats please me," etc.).

Translate the following.

1. *Die Frauen ärgern mich.*

   ....

2. *Er (der Mantel) steht ihr gut.*

   ....

3. *Es ärgert mich.*   ....

4. *Es steht Ihnen gut.*

   ....

5. *Es gefällt mir.*   ....

6. *Sie gefallen mir.*   ....

7. *Wie geht es Ihnen?*

   ....

8. *Es freut mich.*

   ....

9. *Es sieht aus, als ob . . .*

   ....

10. *Es wundert mich.*

....

11. *Es geht mir gut.*

....

12. *Es scheint heute warm zu sein.*

....

13. *Er (sie) tut mir leid.*

....

14. *Es tut mir leid.*

....

Exercise 45

Translate the following words.

1. *Gefahr* ....

2. *Baukunst* ....

3. *Lohn* ....

4. *Gehirn* ....

5. *Insel* ....

6. *Platz* ....

7. *Weltraum* ....

8. *Wissen* ....

9. *Ansager* ....

10. *Pferd* ....

Exercise 46

TRACK 29

The pronoun *es* is often used to mean "there," referring to something countable, definite, and something indefinite, and you use this impersonal pronoun in the passive voice. Don't forget that you may use the indefinite pronoun *man* (one) as the subject of a verb, but only in the singular. Often the verb with *man* as the subject has a passive voice meaning.

Translate the following.

1. *Es klopft.*

   ....

2. *Mir ist warm (Es ist mir warm).*

   ....

3. *Mir ist übel (Es ist mir übel).*

   ....

4. *Es gibt 100 Bilder in diesem Museum.*

   ....

5. *Es gibt viele Fabriken in dieser Stadt.*

   ....

6. *Es fehlen drei Studenten.*

   ....

7. *Es sind meine Freunde.*

   ....

8. *Es wurde nur Russisch gesprochen.*

   ....

9. *Es wird gemacht werden.*

   ....

PART 7: VERBS: SECTION B

10. *Man weiß nicht, was passieren kann.*

....

11. *Man würde das nicht glauben.*

....

12. *Man sagt.*   ....

13. *Das darf man nicht machen.*

....

14. *Man isst viel Pizza in Italien.*

....

15. *Man sah sie oft im Supermarkt.*

....

E Appendix A
Answer Key

Part 1: The Article
Exercise 1

1. *der*   the father
2. *die*   the school
3. *das*   the ship
4. *die*   the mother
5. *das*   the child
6. *der*   the chair

Exercise 2

1. mountain
2. steamer
3. triangle
4. railroad
5. uncle
6. earth
7. flesh
8. airplane
9. question
10. Greek

Exercise 3

1. *das*   the little man
2. *das*   the little man
3. *das*   the miss (little woman)
4. *die*   the card
5. *die*   the woman
6. *das*   the girl (little maid)
7. *der*   the man

Exercise 4

1. to, for the mother   dative
2. the girl   nominative, accusative
3. the father   accusative
4. the girl   accusative, nominative
5. the mother   nominative, accusative
6. of the girl   genitive
7. to/for the father   dative
8. the father   nominative
9. to/for the girl   dative
10. of the mother   genitive
11. the mother   accusative, nominative
12. of the father   genitive

Exercise 5

1. grandmother
2. grandfather
3. circle
4. clock/watch
5. city
6. bull
7. cousin (m.)
8. angle
9. science
10. week

Exercise 6

1. *des Schatzes*
2. *des Fußes*
3. *des Kindes*
4. *des Mannes*

Exercise 7

1. *die*   the girls
2. *den*   to/for the girls
3. *der*   of the mothers
4. *den*   to/for the mothers
5. *die*   the mothers
6. *die*   the mothers
7. *der*   of the fathers
8. *die*   the fathers
9. *die*   the fathers
10. *den*   to/for the fathers
11. *der*   of the girls
12. *die*   the girls

Exercise 8

1. work
2. example
3. dress/skirt; rock music

4. book

5. fork

6. money

7. friend

8. glass

9. coffee

10. cookies

Exercise 9

1. *den* I bought the hat.

2. *dem* He buys the father a hat.

3. *dem* The woman gives a piece of cake to the son.

4. *des* The brother of the father has come.

5. *der* Mr. Zimmermann is the teacher.

6. *der* The father lives in Berlin.

Exercise 10

1. which

2. many a

3. this

4. each

5. such (a)

6. that

Exercise 11

1. life/existence

2. spoon

3. light

4. man/human being/person

5. knife

6. milk

7. chocolate

8. tea

9. plate

10. sugar

Exercise 12

1. *dieser* this man

2. *dieser* to/for this woman

3. *dieses* the child

4. *diesen* this man

5. *diesem* to/for this child

6. *dieses* of this man

7. *diese* this woman

8. *diese* this woman

9. *dieses* this child

10. *dieses* of this child

11. *dieser* of this woman

12. *diesem* to/for this man

Exercise 13

1. sausage

2. veal

3. lamb

4. beef

5. lake

6. ham

7. pork

8. state

9. environment

10. bird

Exercise 14

1. *diese* these men

2. *dieser* of these children

3. *diesen* to/for these children

4. *diesen* to/for these men

5. *diese* these men

6. *diese* these women

7. *dieser* of these men

8. *diese* these children

9. *dieser* of these women

10. *diesen* to/for these women

11. *diese* these children

12. *diese* these women

Exercise 15

1. factory

2. fish

3. bottle

4. vegetables

5. weight
6. pound
7. animal
8. water
9. wine
10. scientist

Exercise 16

1. *ein*   a man
2. *keine*   no men
3. *keine*   no men
4. *keinen*   to/for no men
5. *einem*   to/for a man
6. *eines*   of a man
7. *einen*   a man
8. *keiner*   of no men

Exercise 17

1. comfortable
2. brown
3. invention
4. color
5. liquid
6. researcher
7. ugly
8. idea
9. above/upstairs
10. stairs

Exercise 18

1. *eine*   a woman
2. *keinen*   to/for no women
3. *keine*   no women
4. *keine*   no women
5. *keiner*   of no women
6. *einer*   to/for a woman
7. *eine*   a woman
8. *einer*   of a woman

Exercise 19

1. *keine*   no children
2. *keiner*   of no children
3. *keinen*   to/for no children
4. *keine*   no children
5. *ein*   a child
6. *ein*   a child
7. *eines*   of a child
8. *einem*   to/for a child

Exercise 20

1. suit
2. elevator
3. art
4. air
5. escalator
6. handbag
7. salt
8. department store
9. economic/industrial
10. scientific/scholarly

Exercise 21

1. its
2. your (familiar)
3. her
4. his
5. a
6. my
7. your (polite singular and plural)
8. no
9. our
10. your (familiar plural)
11. their

Exercise 22

1. warmth   *Wärme*
2. process   *Verfahren*
3. clothing   *Kleidung*

4. rocket   *Rakete*
5. political party *Partei*
6. leather   *Leder*
7. overcoat   *Mantel*
8. size   *Größe*
9. following   *folgend*
10. employee   *Angestellte*

Exercise 23

1. *ein (kein, mein, dein, sein, ihr, unser, euer, ihr, Ihr) Mann*
2. *keines   seines   unseres   Ihres*
3. *meinem   ihrem   ihrem*
4. *deinen   eu(e)ren*

Exercise 24

1. *eine (keine, meine, deine, seine, ihre, unsere, euere, ihre, Ihre) Frau*
2. *keiner   deiner   unserer   ihrer*
3. *meiner   seiner   ihrer   Ihrer*
4. *keine   meine   deine   seine   ihre*
    unsere   eur(e)re   ihre   Ihre

Exercise 25

1. briefcase
2. bookstore
3. glove
4. pants
5. jacket
6. buttons
7. motor
8. shirt
9. sunshine
10. submarine

Exercise 26

1. *kein   mein   dein   sein*
    ihr   unser   euer   ihr   Ihr
2. *meines   deines   ihres   eu(e)res   Ihres*
3. *keinem   seinem   unserem   Ihrem*
4. *ein (kein, mein, dein, sein, ihr, unser, euer, ihr, Ihr) Kind*

Exercise 27

1. *keine*
2. *keinen*
3. *keiner*
4. *keine*
5. *keine*
6. *keinen*
7. *keiner*
8. *keine*
9. *keine*
10. *keinen*
11. *keiner*
12. *keine*

Exercise 28

1. letter
2. free
3. history/story
4. necktie
5. sock
6. shoe
7. environment
8. people/nation
9. wash
10. handkerchief

Exercise 29

1. my
2. your (s)
3. his
4. her
5. its
6. our
7. your (pl)
8. their
9. your (polite)

Exercise 30

1. cheap
2. law
3. hard/stiff
4. today
5. classroom
6. new
7. sun
8. rain
9. expensive
10. soft

Exercise 31

1. I
2. you (s, familiar)
3. he
4. she
5. it
6. we
7. you (pl)
8. they
9. you (polite)

Exercise 32

1. broad/wide
2. narrow/tight
3. historical
4. speed/velocity
5. high
6. low
7. obvious
8. rule/direction/instruction
9. Vienna
10. wide

Exercise 33

1. I have my notebook.
2. She has her backpack.
3. We love our grandmother.
4. Our teacher is not here.
5. I do not know your neighbors.

Exercise 34

1. Berlin, July 23rd, 6 . . .
2. School is closed on Saturday.
3. *Heute ist der 15. Juli.*
4. In October it is usually cold.
5. *Wir gehen am Montag zur (zu + der) Bäckerei.*

Exercise 35

1. moment
2. exit
3. population
4. entrance
5. area/region/field
6. immediately/same
7. social
8. position
9. lecture
10. time

Exercise 36

1. her hands
2. *seinen Hut*
3. liberty
4. *Das Leben*

Exercise 37

1. development
2. result
3. luggage
4. suitcase
5. native country
6. homesickness
7. decade
8. soon
9. now
10. calm/quiet

Exercise 38

1. *vor dem Frühstück*
2. They are in school.
3. *zum (zu + dem) Frühstück*

4. after supper
5. little Marcus
6. *Fritz ist klein.*
7. poor Mary
8. *Stephanie ist arm.*
9. *Sie gehen in die Schule.*

Exercise 39

1. bed
2. trip
3. war
4. solution
5. passport
6. red
7. rapid/fast
8. strong
9. dining table
10. table

Exercise 40

1. the Netherlands
2. Slovakia
3. Turkey
4. the United States
5. Switzerland

Exercise 41

1. lightning
2. flower
3. thunder
4. thunderstorm
5. business world
6. rain
7. difficult
8. world
9. weather
10. between

Exercise 42

1. *die meisten Leute*
2. *der Mann und die Frau*
3. my father and mother

Exercise 43

1. eighth
2. first
3. fifth
4. third
5. ninth
6. sixth
7. seventh
8. storm
9. fourth
10. cloud
11. tenth
12. second

Exercise 44

1. My friend is a widow.
2. My mother is an American.
3. *Der junge Mann ist Student.*
4. I have a headache (a toothache).
5. *Er ist ein guter Arzt.*
6. He is a physician.

Exercise 45

1. soon
2. before
3. born
4. memory
5. body
6. notebook
7. right/very
8. as soon as
9. in spite of
10. meeting point

Part 2: The Noun

Exercise 1

1. *den Vater*
2. *dem Vater*
3. *des Vaters*
4. *der Vater*
5. *die Väter*
6. *die Väter*
7. *den Vätern*
8. *der Väter*

Exercise 2

1. *Wagen*
2. *Wagen*
3. *Wagen*
4. *Wagens*
5. *Wagen*
6. *Wagen*
7. *Wagen*
8. *Wagen*

Exercise 3

1. *Mädchen*
2. *Mädchen*
3. *Mädchens*
4. *Mädchen*
5. *Mädchen*
6. *Mädchen*
7. *Mädchen*
8. *Mädchen*

Exercise 4

1. *Bruder*
2. *Bruder*
3. *Bruders*
4. *Bruder*
5. *Brüdern*
6. *Brüder*
7. *Brüder*
8. *Brüder*

Exercise 5

1. *Vogel*
2. *Vogel*
3. *Vogels*
4. *Vogel*
5. *Vögel*
6. *Vögeln*
7. *Vögel*
8. *Vögel*

Exercise 6

1. *Mutter*
2. *Mutter*
3. *Mutter*
4. *Mutter*
5. *Mütter*
6. *Mütter*
7. *Müttern*
8. *Mütter*

Exercise 7

1. *Sohn*
2. *Sohn*
3. *Sohns*
4. *Sohn*
5. *Söhne*
6. *Söhne*
7. *Söhne*
8. *Söhnen*

Exercise 8

1. *Nacht*
2. *Nacht*
3. *Nacht*
4. *Nacht*
5. *Nächten*
6. *Nächte*
7. *Nächte*
8. *Nächte*

Exercise 9

1. *Hand*
2. *Hand*
3. *Hand*
4. *Hand*
5. *Hände*
6. *Händen*
7. *Hände*
8. *Hände*

Exercise 10

1. *Tags*
2. *Tag*
3. *Tag*
4. *Tag*
5. *Tage*
6. *Tage*
7. *Tage*
8. *Tagen*

Exercise 11

1. *Monat*
2. *Monats*
3. *Monat*
4. *Monat*
5. *Monaten*
6. *Monate*
7. *Monate*
8. *Monate*

Exercise 12

1. *Jahr*
2. *Jahr*
3. *Jahrs*
4. *Jahr*
5. *Jahre*
6. *Jahre*
7. *Jahre*
8. *Jahren*

Exercise 13

1. *Hauses*
2. *Haus*
3. *Haus*
4. *Haus*
5. *Land*
6. *Land*
7. *Land*
8. *Landes*

Exercise 14

1. *die Häuser*
2. *die Häuser*
3. *den Häusern*
4. *der Häuser*
5. *die Länder*
6. *die Länder*
7. *der Länder*
8. *den Ländern*

Exercise 15

1. the picture
2. the field
3. the valley
4. the grass
5. the light
6. the people
7. the song
8. the village

Exercise 16

1. the place
2. the forest
3. the dress
4. the word
5. the star
6. the nest
7. the egg
8. the castle

Exercise 17

1. *Schule*
2. *Schule*
3. *Schule*
4. *Schule*
5. *Tasche*
6. *Tasche*
7. *Tasche*
8. *Tasche*

Exercise 18

1. *Schulen*
2. *Schulen*
3. *Schulen*
4. *Schulen*
5. *Taschen*
7. *Taschen*
6. *Taschen*
8. *Taschen*

Exercise 19

1. *Jungen*
2. *Jungen*
3. *Jungen*
4. *Jungen*
5. *Jungen*
6. *Jungen*
7. *Junge*
8. *Jungen*

Exercise 20

1. *Herr*
2. *Herrn*
3. *Herrn*
4. *Herrn*
5. *Herren*
6. *Herren*
7. *Herren*
8. *Herren*

Exercise 21

1. *Studenten*
2. *Studenten*
3. *Studenten*
4. *Studenten*
5. *Student*
6. *Studenten*
7. *Studenten*
8. *Studenten*

Exercise 22

1. *Philosoph*
2. *Philosophen*
3. *Philosophen*
4. *Philosophen*
5. *Philosophen*
6. *Philosophen*
7. *Philosophen*
8. *Philosophen*

Exercise 23

1. the boy
2. the fool
3. the human being
4. Mr. Zimmermann is my friend.
5. the lion
6. the count
7. I am going to Germany with Mr. Zimmermann.
8. the raven

Exercise 24

1. *Schmerz*
2. *Schmerzes*
3. *Schmerz*
4. *Schmerz*
5. *Schmerzen*
6. *Schmerzen*
7. *Schmerzen*
8. *Schmerzen*

Exercise 25

1. *Doktoren*
2. *Doktor*
3. *Doktoren*
4. *Doktoren*
5. *Doktors*
6. *Doktor*
7. *Doktor*
8. *Doktoren*

Exercise 26

1. *Augen*
2. *Augen*
3. *Augen*
4. *Augen*
5. *Auge*
6. *Auge*
7. *Auge*
8. *Auges*

Exercise 27

1. *Studium*
2. *Studien*
3. *Studien*
4. *Studien*
5. *Studien*
6. *Studiums*
7. *Studium*
8. *Studium*

Exercise 28

1. the state
2. the drama
3. the date
4. the ear
5. the neighbor
6. German high school
7. the bed
8. the lake

9. the end
10. the farmer
11. the shirt

Exercise 29

1. *Glauben*
2. *Glauben*
3. *Glauben*
4. *Glauben*
5. *Glauben*
6. *Glauben*
7. *Glaubens*
8. *Glaube*

Exercise 30

1. *Herzen*
2. *Herzen*
3. *Herzen*
4. *Herzen*
5. *Herz*
6. *Herzen*
7. *Herzens*
8. *Herz*

Exercise 31

1. *Willen*
2. *Willen*
3. *Wille*
4. *Willen*
5. *Willens*
6. *Willen*
7. *Willen*
8. *Willen*

Exercise 32

1. *Gedanken*
2. *Gedanken*
3. *Gedanken*

4. *Gedanken*
5. *Gedanken*
6. *Gedankens*
7. *Gedanke*
8. *Gedanken*

Exercise 33

1. *die Hotels*
2. *die Pianos*
3. *die Autos*
4. *die Kinos*

Exercise 34

1. *das Kind*
2. *der Mann*
3. *die Frau*
4. *der Frau*
5. *des Kind(e)s*
6. *des Mannes*
7. *die Kinder*
8. *die Männer*
9. *die Frauen*

Exercise 35

1. Charles's girlfriend is in Germany.
2. Hans's sister is taking a trip through Germany.
3. Mary's hat is lying on the table.
4. George's father is not coming today.
5. Fred and Max's father lives in Munich.

Exercise 36

1. Goethe's works
2. the son of old Mrs. Hausmann
3. the houses of London
4. the works of young Frost
5. the countries of Europe
6. Mrs. Werkmeister's son
7. Europe's poets
8. the large cities of China

Exercise 37

1. Dr. Wenger's daughter
2. the daughter of Dr. Wenger
3. the daughter of the doctor
4. Queen Victoria's campaign
5. the campaign of Queen Victoria
6. the campaign of the queen
7. Maximilian the Great lived in the seventh century.
8. The son of Maximilian the Great was Roland the Pious.
9. They fought against Maximilian the Great.
10. They speak about Maximilian the Great.

Exercise 38

1. *der Lehrer*
2. *der Künstler*
3. the garden
4. the hammer
5. *der Laden*
6. the floor
7. *der Faden*
8. the north
9. the gardener

Exercise 39

1. the afternoon
2. *der Montag*
3. *der Mai*
4. *der König*
5. *der Teppich*
6. the evening
7. the cage
8. the spring
9. the nationalism
10. *der Idealismus*
11. *der Neuling*
12. the summer
13. *der Morgen*

Exercise 40

1. the school
2. *die Rose*
3. the bakery
4. *die Religion*
5. the girl friend
6. *die Tapferkeit*
7. the university
8. *die Zeitung*
9. the relationship
10. *die Schönheit*
11. the nation

Exercise 41

1. the singing
2. (the) silver
3. the dancing
4. (the) copper
5. the girl
6. the study
7. the paper
8. (the) gold
9. the writing
10. the little dog
11. the date

Exercise 42

1. *der Hausherr*
2. the key to the bathroom door (*das Bad* ["the bath"] + *das Zimmer* ["the room"] + *der Schlüssel* ["the key"])
3. *das Schlafzimmer* = the bedroom
4. the oatmeal (*der Hafer* ["oats"] + *die Grütze* ["grits"])

Exercise 43

1. He is my brother's friend.
2. The baby is a girl.
3. The count has no money.

Exercise 44

1. The mother of the children is in Switzerland.
2. The colleague of my sister is called Michael.
3. Madrid is the capital of Spain.
4. The airport of Frankfurt is well known.
5. In spite of his exam, he is going to the rock concert.
6. One day he gave us a call.
7. One evening he came into my apartment.

Exercise 45

1. Jens came from his room.
2. Jens works at McDonald's.
3. The doctor is with the patient.
4. The teacher talks to him.
5. We'll go to Salzburg tomorrow.
6. Jens is just returning from the market.
7. We'll go to the beach today.

Exercise 46

1. to answer
2. *folgen*
3. resemble
4. *begegnen*
5. please
6. *helfen*
7. thank
8. *gehören*
9. fit/suit
10. *dienen*
11. obey
12. *schaden*

Exercise 47

1. I will be in Stuttgart till the end of August.
2. We went to the theater without our brother.
3. We walked through town.
4. Here is a letter for you.
5. The whole world is against me.
6. I will take care of you.

Exercise 48

1. *Gute Nacht!*
2. Best regards!
3. They have already been in South America a month.
4. Good morning!
5. *Wir haben den ganzen Tag gearbeitet.*
6. This winter, I am going to America.

Part 3: The Pronoun

Exercise 1

1. him   her   it
2. of me
3. to you
4. I
5. you
6. you
7. he   she   it
8. me
9. of you
10. to me
11. of him   of her   of it
12. to him   to her   to it

Exercise 2

1. you
2. to you
3. of them   of you
4. we
5. they   you
6. you
7. us
8. they   you
9. of us
10. of you
11. to us
12. to them   to you

Exercise 3

1. *Er grüßt sie.*
2. *Der Vater grüßt die Frau.*
3. *Sie geht mit ihm.*
4. *Der Sohn geht mit dem Vater.*

Exercise 4

1. The carpet is red.
2. It is red.
3. The father sees the clock.
4. He sees it.
5. The woman gives a teddy bear to the child.
6. She gives it to him.

Exercise 5

1. Do you know the girl?
2. Do you know her?
3. They are speaking with the boy.
4. They are speaking with him.

Exercise 6

1. She writes with the felt-tip.
2. She writes with it.
3. The schoolboys are playing with the tennis balls.
4. They are playing with them.
5. They knew about the theory of relativity.
6. They knew about it.
7. He is sitting on the sofa.
8. He is sitting on it.
9. She has the handbag.
10. She has it.

Exercise 7

1. *Sie denken an die schöne Fahrt.*
   They are thinking of the beautiful trip.
2. *Sie denken daran.*
   They are thinking of it.
3. *Sie denken an den Freund.*
   They are thinking of their friend.
4. *Sie denken an ihn.*
   They are thinking of him.

Exercise 8

1. you are glad
2. we are glad
3. they are glad
4. to be glad
5. you are glad
6. I am glad
7. he is glad
8. you are glad

Exercise 9

1. *Sie waschen sich*   you wash yourself
2. *sie waschen sich*   they wash themselves
3. *wir waschen uns*   we wash ourselves
4. *ich wasche mich*   I wash myself
5. *sich waschen*   to wash oneself
6. *du wäschst dich*   you wash yourself
7. *er wäscht sich*   he washes himself
8. *ihr wascht euch*   you wash yourselves

Exercise 10

1. to be interested
2. to be glad
3. to sit down

Exercise 11

1. *helfen*   they help themselves
2. *helfen*   you help yourselves
3. *hilft*   he helps himself
4. *helfen*   we help ourselves
5. *helfe*   I help myself
6. *hilfst*   you help yourself
7. *helft*   you help yourself

Exercise 12

1. You wash your socks.
2. You wash your socks.
3. They wash their socks.

4. I wash my socks.
5. He washes his socks.
6. You wash your socks.
7. We wash our socks.

Exercise 13

1. She buys a blouse for her.
2. She buys a blouse for herself.

Exercise 14

1. *Sie machen sich das Mittagessen.*
   They make their own lunch.
2. *Sie sehen sich oft.*
   They often see each other.
3. *Sie machen sich das Mittagessen selbst.*
   They make their lunch themselves.
4. *Sie hat es selbst gesagt.*
   She has said it herself.

Exercise 15

1. <u>Take</u> my sweater! Thank you, I <u>have</u> mine.
2. Your office <u>is</u> larger than ours.
3. She <u>needs</u> her pencil and I mine.
4. He <u>writes</u> with his pen and she <u>writes</u> with hers.
5. <u>Is</u> that your umbrella, Mr. Werkmeister? No, that <u>is</u> not mine, it <u>is</u> yours.
6. Whose child is she <u>calling</u>, his or yours?

Exercise 16

1. *War es dieses Restaurant? Nein, es war jenes.*
   Was it this restaurant? No, it was that one.
2. *Dieses Geschäftshaus ist hoch, jenes ist nicht so hoch.*
   This office building is high, that one is not so high.
3. *Dieser hat es nicht getan sondern jener.*
   This one did not do it but that one did.

Exercise 17

1. He did not do it.
2. Those cannot be helped.
3. Those are my cousins.
4. This is my pupil.
5. I am not able to give it to him.

Exercise 18

1. *dieselben*
2. *dasselbe*
3. *dieselben*
4. *desselben*
5. *denselben*
6. *demselben*
7. *derselben*
8. *derselbe*
9. *denselben*
10. *desselben*
11. *dieselbe*
12. *demselben*
13. *derselben*
14. *derselbe*
15. *dasselbe*
16. *dieselbe*

Exercise 19

1. To whom have you given the cake?
2. What did he tell you yesterday?
3. With whom are you speaking?
4. Whom do you see?
5. Whose piano is this?
6. whose
7. who
8. to whom or for whom
9. what
10. whom
11. Who is that?
12. what

Exercise 20

1. *Mit wem sprechen Sie? Ich spreche mit meinem Mechaniker.*
   With whom are you speaking? I am speaking with my mechanic.
2. *Wovon sprachen Sie? Wir sprachen von dem neuen Drama.*
   Of what were you talking? We were talking about the new drama.
3. *An wen denken Sie? Ich denke an meine Tochter in Schweden.*
   Of whom are you thinking? I am thinking of my daughter in Sweden.
4. *Woran denken Sie? Ich denke an den schönen gestrigen Tag.*
   Of what are you thinking? I am thinking of the beautiful day yesterday.

Exercise 21

1. What kind of envelopes do you have there?
2. *ein*   What kind of girl is she?
3. *einem*   In what kind of train do you travel?

Exercise 22

1. that/which
2. of which
3. to which
4. whom/which
5. to whom
6. whom
7. whom
8. to whom, to which
9. who
10. that/which
11. who
12. whose
13. whose/of which
14. who/which
15. to whom
16. whose

Exercise 23

1. The woman who is standing there is named Kühn.
2. The man, whose son I know, lives here.
3. That is the child to whom she gave the ring.
4. The coat that he is wearing today is new.
5. The mirror he is standing at belongs to me.
6. The men with whom I spoke yesterday are my fellow students.
7. The boy who cannot finish the reading today must come again tomorrow.

Exercise 24

1. *welchen*
2. *deren*
3. *welcher*
4. *welches*
5. *welche*
6. *welcher*
7. *welche*
8. *welche*
9. *welche*
10. *deren*
11. *welches*
12. *dessen*
13. *dessen*
14. *welchen*
15. *welchem*
16. *welchem*

Exercise 25

1. That is the most beautiful thing (that) I have ever had.
2. what/whatever/that
3. Whatever I possess belongs to you.
4. He who lies once is never believed.
5. what/whatever/that
6. he who/whoever
7. All (that) she has heard about it is correct.
8. whomever/whom
9. whose
10. whomever/to whom
11. I don't know whom to believe.

Exercise 26

1. People drink a lot of wine in France.
2. You should not say things like that.
3. Did you hear/learn anything new?
4. No, I have not read anything new.
5. Today there was nothing interesting in the news.
6. Tell me something nice.
7. He gives him something that he can easily afford.
8. Tell me something (that) I have not yet heard.
9. She believes nothing he says.
10. That is something very silly.
11. I must have something delicious.

Exercise 27

1. Why do you speak to everyone?
2. That is nobody's business.
3. That is not everyone's concern.
4. I am hearing someone's voice.
5. Someone is talking outside.
6. The bath towel belongs to no one.
7. Not everybody can go to South America.

Exercise 28

1. Are both going to Bavaria?
2. The parents of both (of them) have died.
3. Each has its good points.
4. Neither one of the two is going to the discotheque.
5. Each one has his own taste.
6. One of the children has an apple.
7. Did you speak to one of them?
8. One of them must be right.
9. They said nobody had done it.
10. I am not able to deal with anyone now.

Exercise 29

1. The opinion of many is not always correct.
2. A true friendship is possible with a few only.
3. A little will suffice.
4. You accomplished a lot.
5. She can make much out of little.
6. He has experienced little.

Exercise 30

1.	*alles*	All that glitters is not gold.
2.	*allen*	No, we cannot go with all (of them).
3.	*Alles*	I give you everything.
4.	*alle*	Regards from me to all (of them).
5.	*Alles*	He is my one and all.
6.	*alles*	That is all (that) I have.

Part 4: Prepositions, Adverbs, and Conjunctions
Exercise 1

1. We travel to (as far as) Prague.
2. Wait till next Tuesday.
3. I have no money until the second.
4. She is going through the park.
5. This present is for you.
6. What do you have against the woman?
7. They went to the art museum without the sister.
8. They rode around the city with the bus.
9. Whoever is not for me is against me.

Exercise 2

1. flood
2. reason/use
3. cause
4. surprise
5. funny
6. state
7. citizen
8. welcome
9. customs

Exercise 3

1. He is at the hairdresser.
2. She is living at her uncle's house.
3. Oxford is close to London.
4. He is at work.
5. He was beside himself with anger.
6. All were there except my brother.
7. He is drinking from a bottle.
8. She comes out of the room.

Exercise 4

1. business trip
2. pleasure trip
3. arrival
4. formal
5. guest
6. France
7. home
8. brave
9. descendant
10. basis

Exercise 5

1. I am going to my aunt's (house).
2. A poem by the German poet Goethe
3. Today I must go to the doctor.
4. After dinner he's going out.
5. Come home with me.
6. When are you going to France?
7. I have not seen her since August 1.
8. This present is from me.
9. The capital of America

Exercise 6

1. Where are you walking? (lit. Where do you take a walk?) I am walking in the park. (lit. I take a walk in the park.)
2. Where is the pen? It is lying on the writing table.
3. Where are the girls playing? They are playing in the living room.

Exercise 7

1. east
2. tree
3. meadow
4. area/surface
5. forest
6. green
7. pretty/nice
8. enormous
9. window
10. minute

Exercise 8

1. The woman is carrying the picture into the living room.
2. Where are the women going? The women are going into the park.
3. Where does he place (lit. lay) the knife? He is placing (lit. laying) it on the table.

Exercise 9

1. train station
2. straight ahead
3. conductor
4. necessary things
5. once again
6. Black Forest cake
7. annual
8. change/variation
9. important/significant
10. precipitation

Exercise 10

1. She is standing at the gate. He is going to the gate.
2. The frying pan is sitting (lit. standing) on the shelf.
3. She places the frying pan on the stove.
4. He is dancing behind me.
5. He places himself behind me.
6. They are in the swimming pool.
7. They are coming into the inn.

Exercise 11

1. amount
2. inhabitant
3. kitchen
4. bathroom
5. garage
6. room
7. dining room
8. living room
9. bedroom

Exercise 12

1. Among the guests are many Spaniards.
2. Under the writing desk is the wastebasket.
3. He puts the telegram under the envelope.
4. He sits down next to his aunt.
5. He is sitting next to his aunt.
6. I am hanging the light over the piano.
7. A lamp is hanging over the piano.
8. A German teacher is living above him.

Exercise 13

1. kitchen
2. towel
3. soap
4. apartment
5. chimney
6. pope
7. springtime
8. medieval
9. holy
10. poem

Exercise 14

1. He sits down between my sister and me.
2. He is sitting between my sister and me.
3. A year ago he went to Italy.
4. She is going in front of the closet.
5. She is standing in front of the closet.

Exercise 15

1. During the day she works in a private bank.
2. I could not go out because of my headache.
3. Instead of my father, my brother went to the concert.
4. In spite of the bad weather, he did not stay home.

Exercise 16

1. poetry
2. victorious

3. metropolis
4. achievement
5. power
6. piano
7. roof
8. balcony
9. closet
10. furniture

Exercise 17

1. below
2. above
3. on this side of
4. for the sake of
5. outside of
6. on the other side of
7. inside of/within

Exercise 18

1. We visited our grandmother in order to see her new dog.
2. He left the room without looking around.
3. Instead of going to the theater, he visited his uncle.

Exercise 19

1. picture
2. lamp
3. mirror
4. store
5. famous
6. weakness
7. party
8. protection
9. capital
10. seat

Exercise 20

1. *am*
2. *aufs*
3. *ins*

4. *im*
5. *zur*
6. *vom*
7. *am*
8. *ans*
9. *zum*

Exercise 21

1. the quick man
2. The man works quickly.
3. She walks very slowly.
4. She will soon be here.
5. He likes her very much.
6. They like to go dancing.
7. I like to crochet.

Exercise 22

1. figure/illustration
2. construction/building
3. bread
4. narrow/close
5. explanation
6. price
7. purchase
8. go shopping
9. Europe
10. United States

Exercise 23

1. Fortunately, he did not come so early.
2. At night he sleeps.
3. wisely
4. customarily, in the accustomed way
5. strangely, singularly
6. unfortunately

Exercise 24

1. street
2. avenue
3. church

4. park
5. film
6. subway station
7. opinion
8. page, side
9. stream, current
10. work

Exercise 25

1. Either we go immediately or we will arrive too late.
2. either . . . or
3. She is not dumb, but lazy.
4. She isn't going to Germany, but rather is taking a tour through Spain.
5. He did not buy the airline ticket because he did not have enough money.
6. She has a ticket for the theater, but she cannot go.
7. but
8. We must hurry or we will miss the bus.
9. and
10. or
11. for
12. but (on the contrary)

Exercise 26

1. Vienna
2. manager
3. department
4. salary
5. colleague
6. post office
7. hospital
8. policeman
9. bus
10. subway

Exercise 27

1. how/as
2. before
3. although
4. since
5. in case

6. whether
7. that
8. when/than, as
9. as if
10. though
11. before
12. while

Exercise 28

1. order
2. bill/check
3. tip
4. silverware
5. dishes
6. menu
7. dessert
8. main course
9. fork
10. knife

Exercise 29

1. when/if
2. after
3. in order that
4. the (+ comparative) the (+ comparative)
5. while
6. when
7. until
8. where
9. since (reason), as
10. because

Exercise 30

1. ground, soil, floor
2. federation, union
3. big city
4. scarcely
5. independent
6. responsibility
7. behavior

8. television set
9. radio set
10. police station

Exercise 31

1. He does it now because he has no more time to do it later.
2. Don't wait any longer since he will not be coming (anymore) today.
3. He recognized him, although he had not seen him for forty years.
4. I know that he is not home today.

Exercise 32

1. restaurant
2. bill
3. gravy/sauce
4. cabbage
5. salad
6. plate
7. knife
8. fork
9. tablespoon
10. soup

Exercise 33

1. When I met him yesterday, he was wearing a silver glove.
2. When he was in London, he often went to the theater.
3. She lived in Austria when she was old.
4. When are you coming to the language lab today?
5. Tell me when you will come to the store today.
6. I don't know when I will come to the office today.
7. When I see him, I will let him know.
8. Whenever she came home, she always drank a hot chocolate.
9. Whenever he was in Cologne, he visited the Cathedral.
10. When I am (lit. shall be) in Wuppertal, I will visit your grandmother.

Exercise 34

1. roast
2. vegetable
3. potato
4. dessert
5. fruits
6. Middle Ages
7. night
8. dead
9. solid, firm, permanent
10. Greek

Exercise 35

1. Perhaps he will come anyway (lit. anyhow).
2. Partly she cannot come, partly she does not want to.
3. Her sister-in-law is ill; therefore she cannot come.
4. She seldom comes now; at that time she came often.

Part 5: The Adjective
Exercise 1

1. *Das Mädchen schreibt gut.*	The girl writes well.
2. *Der Junge liest gut.*	The boy reads well.
3. *Das Münchener Eis ist teuer.*	Munich ice cream is expensive.
4. *Der Film ist gut.*	The film is good.
5. *Das Buch ist gut.*	The book is good.
6. *Sie wird alt.*	She is getting old.
7. *ein Berliner Theater*	a Berlin theater
8. *Er wird alt.*	He is getting old.

Exercise 2

1. The diligent student reads a book.
2. An interesting article is in the newspaper.

Exercise 3

1. *guter*
2. *guten*
3. *gutem*

4. *guten*
5. *gute*
6. *guter*
7. *guter*
8. *gute*
9. *gutem*
10. *gutes*
11. *gutes*
12. *guten*

Exercise 4

1. *gute*
2. *guten*
3. *guter*
4. *gute*
5. *guter*
6. *gute*
7. *guten*
8. *gute*
9. *gute*
10. *guten*
11. *guter*
12. *gute*

Exercise 5

1. the good father
2. of the good father
3. to or for the good father
4. the good father
5. the good mother
6. of the good mother
7. to or for the good mother
8. the good mother
9. the good child
10. of the good child
11. to or for the good child
12. the good child

Exercise 6

1. *guten*
2. *guten*
3. *guten*
4. *guten*
5. *guten*
6. *guten*
7. *guten*
8. *guten*
9. *guten*
10. *guten*
11. *guten*
12. *guten*

Exercise 7

1. *guter*
2. *guten*
3. *guten*
4. *guten*
5. *gute*
6. *guten*
7. *gute*
8. *guten*
9. *guten*
10. *gutes*
11. *gutes*
12. *guten*

Exercise 8

1. *guten*
2. *guten*
3. *guten*
4. *guten*
5. *guten*
6. *guten*
7. *guten*
8. *guten*
9. *guten*
10. *guten*
11. *guten*
12. *guten*

Exercise 9

1. *dem*
2. *den*
3. *des*
4. *der*
5. *der*
6. *die*
7. *der*
8. *die*
9. *das*
10. *des*
11. *das*
12. *dem*

Exercise 10

1. *den*
2. *Fremden*
3. *die Fremden*
4. *die*
5. *den*
6. *die*
7. *der*
8. *die Alten*
9. *Kleinen*
10. *Kleinen*
11. *die*
12. *die Kleinen*

Exercise 11

1. the tall one
2. the good one
3. *ein*
4. *ein*
5. *ein*

Exercise 12

1. *am ärmsten*
2. *ärmer*
3. *arm*
4. *jünger*
5. *jung*

6. *am jüngsten*
7. *am längsten*
8. *lang*
9. *länger*

Exercise 13

1. *am reichsten*
2. *reicher*
3. *reich*
4. *langsamer*
5. *am langsamsten*
6. *langsam*

Exercise 14

1. *am heißesten*
2. *heißer*
3. *heiß*
4. *kürzer*
5. *am kürzesten*
6. *kurz*
7. *am mildesten*
8. *mild*
9. *milder*
10. *alt*
11. *älter*
12. *am ältesten*
13. *am weitesten*
14. *weiter*
15. *weit*

Exercise 15

1. *am dunkelsten*
2. *dunkler*
3. *dunkel*
4. *saurer*
5. *am sauersten*
6. *sauer*
7. *selten*
8. *seltner*
9. *am seltensten*

Exercise 16

1. Johann is taller than my brother-in-law.
2. She is not as tall as he is.
3. Johann is as tall as my father-in-law.

Exercise 17

1. *am meisten*
2. *am nächsten*
3. *mehr*
4. *nah*
5. *näher*
6. *viel*
7. *am größten*
8. *größer*
9. *groß*
10. *am besten*
11. *gut*
12. *besser*
13. *höher*
14. *hoch*
15. *am höchsten*

Exercise 18

1. *Sie hat viel gegessen.*   She ate a lot (much).
2. *viele Kinder*   many children
3. *das hohe Hotel*   the tall hotel
4. *Das Hotel ist hoch.*   The hotel is tall.

Exercise 19

1. What am I going to do with this little money?
2. Few children are playing on the playground today.
3. He has little time.
4. She has little money.

Exercise 20

1. my favorite brother (lit. my most liked brother)
2. She likes to sing.
3. I am leaving earlier.
4. I take the earlier train.

Exercise 21

1. In December the days are the shortest.
2. In December the days become the shortest.
3. She gets prettier every day.
4. The son is younger, but the mother is wiser.

Exercise 22

1. *älterer*
2. *jüngeren*
3. *kleinsten*
4. *kleinstes*
5. *jüngeren*
6. *jüngere*
7. *ältesten*
8. *kleinste*
9. *ältesten*
10. *älterer*
11. *kleinsten*

Exercise 23

1. Johann writes better.
2. Hans writes well.
3. But Lois writes best.
4. my best friend
5. This book is best.
6. the most beautiful girl
7. The mother is most beautiful.
8. This book is the best one.

Exercise 24

1. *dreizehn* (13)
2. *neunzehn* (19)
3. *sechzehn* (17)
4. *siebzehn* (16)
5. *sechzig* (60)
6. *siebzig* (70)
7. *zwanzig* (20)
8. *dreißig* (30)
9. *die Null*

10. *die Million*
11. *die Milliarde*
12. *ein Uhr*
13. *Es ist ein Uhr.*

Exercise 25

1. twenty times
2. three times
3. ten times
4. once
5. thousand times
6. four times
7. twice
8. hundred times

Exercise 26

1. What is today's date? (lit. The how many is today?)
2. Today is the third of July.
3. Chicago, October 19, 1939 . . .
4. Yesterday was the 12th of November.
5. He was born on the 12th of August.
6. Goethe was born on August 28, 1749.
7. the twelfth chapter
8. firstly
9. secondly
10. thirdly

Exercise 27

1. three-fourths
2. two-eighths
3. two and a half
4. He gave her half a Euro.
5. one-twentieth
6. one-eighth
7. one and a half
8. three and a half

Exercise 28

1. Once a week she goes to the movies.
2. I have been to her house three times already.
3. $66 \div 6 = 11$

4. $20 + 14 = 34$
5. $8 \times 9 = 72$
6. $52 - 7 = 45$

Exercise 29

1. at one o'clock
2. at six o'clock
3. It is one.
4. It is twelve.
5. a quarter past four
6. half past four
7. a quarter to five
8. a quarter past five
9. a quarter to five
10. ten after ten
11. five minutes to eleven
12. a quarter past five
13. 6:20 p.m.
14. 12 o'clock midnight

Exercise 30

1. five kilometers
2. two pots of coffee
3. two cups of milk
4. one mile
5. one pot of coffee
6. four meters
7. two liters of beer
8. a liter of beer
9. one glass of milk
10. one meter
11. one cup of milk
12. two glasses of milk

Exercise 31

1. one penny
2. ten pennies
3. three pounds
4. twenty euros
5. one euro
6. one pound

Part 6: Verbs: Section A
Exercise 1

1. they are
2. it is
3. you are
4. you are
5. he is
6. I am
7. you are
8. she is
9. we are

Exercise 2

1. you have
2. you have
3. we have
4. they have
5. I have
6. he has
7. she has
8. you have
9. it has

Exercise 3

1. they become
2. you become
3. she becomes
4. I become
5. you become
6. he becomes
7. it becomes
8. you become
9. we become

Exercise 4

1. it was
2. they were
3. you were
4. you were
5. I was
6. you were

7. he was
8. she was
9. we were

Exercise 5

1. it had
2. you had
3. we had
4. they had
5. you had
6. you had
7. I had
8. she had
9. he had

Exercise 6

1. they became
2. she became
3. we became
4. you became
5. you became
6. he became
7. you became
8. I became
9. it became

Exercise 7

1. he has become
2. he has had
3. he has been
4. you have had
5. you have become
6. I have become
7. you have been
8. I have had
9. I have been

Exercise 8

1. we have become
2. they have had
3. you have had

4. you have become
5. they have become
6. we have been
7. you have been
8. you have had
9. we have had
10. you have become
11. they have been
12. you have been

Exercise 9

1. he had become
2. he had been
3. he had had
4. you had become
5. you had had
6. I had become
7. I had been
8. you had been
9. I had had

Exercise 10

1. we had been
2. we had had
3. we had become
4. you had been
5. you had had
6. you had become
7. they had been
8. they had had
9. they had become
10. you had been
11. you had had
12. you had become

Exercise 11

1. he shall (will) become
2. he shall (will) have
3. you shall (will) become
4. he shall (will) be
5. you shall (will) have
6. you shall (will) be

7. I shall (will) become
8. I shall (will) have
9. I shall (will) be

Exercise 12

1. you shall (will) have
2. you shall (will) be
3. they shall (will) become
4. they shall (will) be
5. they shall (will) have
6. you shall (will) become
7. we shall (will) be
8. we shall (will) become
9. you shall (will) have
10. we shall (will) have
11. you shall (will) become
12. you shall (will) be

Exercise 13

1. he shall have become
2. you shall have had
3. you shall have become
4. he shall have had
5. I shall have become
6. you shall have been
7. I shall have had
8. I shall have been
9. he shall have been

Exercise 14

1. we shall have been
2. we shall have had
3. we shall have become
4. you shall have been
5. you shall have had
6. you shall have become
7. they shall have been
8. they shall have had
9. they shall have become
10. you shall have been
11. you shall have had
12. you shall have become

Exercise 15

1. sprung
2. to spring
3. sprang
4. followed
5. to follow
6. followed

Exercise 16

1. gone
2. he sits
3. lived
4. you sit
5. he travels
6. I sit
7. you travel
8. to sit (strong verb)
9. I travel
10. to travel (weak verb)

Exercise 17

1. *Wir gehen in die Kirche.*
   We are going to church.
2. *Er antwortet ihr.*
   He answers her.
3. *Er erwartet seinen Lehrer.*
   He is expecting his teacher.
4. *Er liest den Empfehlungsbrief.*
   He reads the letter of recommendation.

Exercise 18

1. to help
2. to belong
3. to meet
4. to be missing
5. to please
6. to believe
7. to answer
8. to seem

Exercise 19

1. to serve

2. to happen
3. He helps his mother-in-law.
4. He does not answer her.
5. to fit
6. to follow
7. They met the poet.
8. to thank

Exercise 20

1. She went on (lit. has made) a bicycle tour.
2. He read (lit. has read) the novel.
3. He had read the article.
4. He will have read the news.
5. She was able (lit. has been able) to try the food.
6. She had sat down.
7. He had combed his hair (lit. himself).
8. He has answered (or answered) her.
9. She helped (lit. has helped) his daughter.
10. They had played well all day long.

Exercise 21

1. She died last month.
2. I stayed (lit. had remained) at home.
3. He had not come.
4. We met (lit. have met) in the street yesterday [that is, walking toward each other].
5. Where were you (lit. have you been) last night?
6. The dog had followed his master.
7. We fell (lit. have fallen) asleep late.
8. He went (lit. has gone) to the post office.

Exercise 22

1. I shall have seen her.
2. They will have come tomorrow.
3. They will come today.
4. I shall see her.

Exercise 23

1. He has already been waiting half an hour for him.
2. I have known him for two years.
3. How long have you known John?
4. How long has she been living here?
5. He has been in the United States for ten years.

6. When are you going to Switzerland?
7. I am going next fall.
8. They are going downtown (lit. into the city) today.

Exercise 24

1. She worked many hours in the office before she came home.
2. She drank a lot of milk.
3. She was writing a check when he entered the room.
4. He often visited us before he moved to Hamburg.
5. I met Mr. Zimmermann in the street yesterday, and we talked with each other for a while.

Exercise 25

1. I bought a coat for myself last month.
2. Rilke wrote many lyrical poems.

Exercise 26

1. He had spoken to his son already.
2. She had finished writing the check when he entered the room.

Exercise 27

1. She has probably overslept.
2. The telephone number is probably wrong.
3. They are probably late again.

Exercise 28

1. to tear
2. to understand
3. to break (completely)
4. to use
5. to forgive
6. to mistreat
7. to visit
8. to recognize
9. to receive, get
10. to please
11. to expect
12. to originate
13. to receive, welcome
14. to distrust

Exercise 29

1. you will understand
2. they will have understood
3. recognized
4. originated
5. we had understood
6. forgiven
7. I understand
8. he has understood
9. you understood

Exercise 30

1. She will get up at five o'clock tomorrow.
2. I know (that) she has to get up at five o'clock every day.
3. She will have gotten up at five o'clock tomorrow.
4. She planned not to get up at five o'clock tomorrow.
5. Get up at five o'clock every day!
6. She gets up at five o'clock every day.
7. She got up at five o'clock every day.

Exercise 31

1. I looked through my bag (pocket).
2. She tore the letter apart and threw it away.
3. The train runs nonstop to Hamburg.
4. A (feeling of) great relief is running through the crowd.
5. She dodges my question.
6. Silly rumors are circulating.
7. This includes the whole department store chain.
8. This had included all ten banks.
9. She crosses on a ferry.
10. She crossed by canoe.
11. She translates from Icelandic.
12. She has translated from Norwegian.

Exercise 32

1. *Der Mann holt den Ball wieder.*
   The man fetches the ball back.
2. *Sie hat das Wort wiederholt.*
   She has repeated the word.
3. *Sie wiederholt das Wort.*
   She repeats the word.
4. *Er hat sie unterbrochen.*
   He has interrupted her.

5. *Er bringt sie im Hotel unter.*
   He puts her up in a hotel.
6. *Sie unterstützen ihn.*
   They support him.
7. *Er hat sie unterstützt.*
   He has supported her.
8. *Der Mann holt den Fernsehapparat wieder.*
   The man is bringing the television set back.

Exercise 33

1. the walking child
2. the beloved mother
3. the singing bird
4. singing
5. a walking child
6. the coming and going
7. the singing
8. the dancing
9. loving
10. the loving mother
11. going
12. the vision

Exercise 34

1. written
2. the written matter (something that has been written)
3. beloved
4. the beloved one
5. the lovers (loving ones)
6. to love
7. to travel
8. the traveler

Exercise 35

1. That is easily learned.
2. Much can be seen here.
3. She came into the dining room without seeing (lit. to see) me.
4. She goes to the bank to (lit. in order to) change money.
5. She stayed until ten o'clock instead of going home.

Exercise 36

1. Go! (to a person addressed by *Sie*, singular and plural)

2. Go! (to a person addressed by *du*)
3. Go! (to a person addressed by *ihr*)

Exercise 37

1. Wait!
2. Find!
3. Open!
4. Give!
5. Read!
6. Take!
7. See!
8. Carry!
9. Run!

Exercise 38

1. to get dressed
2. Get dressed!
3. Get up!
4. Be glad!
5. to get up, rise
6. Wash your hands!

Exercise 39

1. have to/must
2. to want/will
3. to be able/can
4. may/to like
5. to be permitted/may
6. shall/ought to

Exercise 40

1. want
2. should
3. must
4. to like
5. can
6. may

Exercise 41

1. you can
2. we can
3. they can
4. you can

5. he can
6. I may
7. he may
8. you may
9. we may
10. I can
11. they may
12. you may

Exercise 42

1. you must
2. they must
3. you must
4. we must
5. he must
6. I like to
7. he likes to
8. you like to
9. you like to
10. we like to
11. I must
12. they like to

Exercise 43

1. I shall have been able
2. I had been able
3. I shall be able
4. I could
5. I have been able

Exercise 44

1. *dürfen* ("to be permitted")
2. *durfte*
3. *darf*
4. *gedurft dürfen*
5. *können* ("to be able")
6. *konnte*
7. *kann*
8. *gekonnt können*
9. *müssen* ("to have to")
10. *gemusst müssen*
11. *muss*
12. *musste*

Exercise 45

1. *mochte*
2. *gemocht mögen*
3. *mögen* ("to like")
4. *mag*
5. *sollte*
6. *gesollt sollen*
7. *sollen* ("shall")
8. *soll*
9. *gewollt wollen*
10. *wollen* ("to want, will")
11. *will*
12. *wollte*

Part 7: Verbs: Section B
Exercise 1

1. He cannot stand it any longer.
2. She must go (away).
3. He wanted (to do) it.
4. Did he really want to write the book?
5. No, she cannot do it.
6. She can speak Japanese.
7. Can she do the work?
8. He wants to come tomorrow.

Exercise 2

1. grateful
2. South America
3. office
4. business
5. credit
6. birthday
7. accident
8. mixture
9. speaker
10. salt

Exercise 3

1. She has learned to speak Japanese.
2. He did not want to come tomorrow.
3. He did not like her.
4. She had been able to do it.
5. He has been wanting to do it.
6. She has been able to do it.

Exercise 4

1. feeling
2. reality
3. past
4. dream
5. moral
6. owner
7. unmarried
8. neck
9. comb
10. sign

Exercise 5

1. I know that she could not (lit. has not been able to) come today.
2. She could not do it.
3. She has not been able to go.
4. She cannot go.

Exercise 6

1. wife
2. male hairdresser
3. grocery store
4. haircut
5. manicure
6. mysterious
7. field/area
8. discovery
9. iron
10. power/force/strength

Exercise 7

1. He is having (lit. is letting) a suit made.
2. Have you had (lit. let) this jacket made in London?
3. I have never heard him laugh.
4. to let
5. He goes shopping.
6. to help
7. He went shopping.
8. to go/walk
9. to hear
10. She has helped her carry the bag.

11. She helped her carry the suitcase.

Exercise 8

1. origin
2. lecture
3. flight
4. biography
5. statement/assertion
6. razor
7. hair
8. brush
9. charming
10. tear

Exercise 9

1. He would like to go to the cinema.
2. That may be false.
3. He likes her.
4. He does not like her.
5. They would like to go to China.
6. May I ask a question?
7. She cannot go to the concert.
8. Can you dance?
9. She could not sing.
10. May she open the door?

Exercise 10

1. foreigner
2. police
3. paper
4. pen
5. calendar
6. page
7. earth
8. health
9. pure/clean
10. tourism

Exercise 11

1. Every child must go to kindergarten at the age of five.
2. I had to sew yesterday.
3. You must not believe that.

4. You should visit your Father and Mother.
5. We ought to meet him at the cinema today.
6. She should cook a German dish.
7. She is known to be very clever.
8. They are supposed to be in Europe.
9. She wants to learn Polish.
10. He did not want to see her again.
11. I intended to do it, but I had no time.
12. He was about to (lit. intended to) leave, when she came.
13. She claims to be educated.
14. She claimed to have been the one.

Exercise 12

1. search
2. airplane
3. translation
4. legislation
5. soldier
6. stamp
7. envelope
8. sale
9. blouse
10. skirt, dress

Exercise 13

1. they knew
2. you know
3. we know
4. you knew
5. they know
6. we knew
7. you know
8. I knew
9. he knows
10. you knew
11. I know
12. he knew

Exercise 14

1. sweater
2. umbrella
3. pink
4. blue
5. white
6. gray
7. knowledge
8. neighbor
9. immigrant
10. black

Exercise 15

1. I know Bern.
2. Do you know Mr. Jacobs?
3. Are you able to lift the chair?
4. I am able to speak Chinese.
5. He is not able to cook.
6. She knows when the celebration begins.
7. She knows that your name is Katherine.

Exercise 16

1. employee
2. cell
3. voice
4. cross
5. success
6. growth
7. complete/perfect
8. fried egg
9. hole
10. sympathetic

Exercise 17

1. She does not let me watch television.
2. Leave me alone!
3. She had a doctor come.
4. I am going to have a dress made.
5. She had a bottle of water brought to her.
6. That can easily be imagined.

Exercise 18

1. folksy
2. castle
3. border/boundary
4. battle
5. acquaintance
6. composition

7. nevertheless
8. average
9. deep/low
10. course

Exercise 19

1. cook
2. secret
3. steel
4. strong
5. part
6. width, latitude
7. pressure
8. degree of latitude
9. boiling point
10. observation

Exercise 20

1. Yesterday there was much laughing and singing.
2. Finnish is spoken here.
3. The title of the book has been mentioned by the author.
4. Can one swim in the Rhine River?
5. One should always speak one's mind.
6. The old people are being helped by the children.
7. The children help the old people.
8. You had not been invited.
9. The author mentions the title of the book.
10. One did not invite you.

Exercise 21

1. old man
2. life span
3. newborn
4. disease
5. increase
6. examination
7. source/spring
8. rule
9. piece
10. increase

Exercise 22

1. The church is being built.

2. The wall is built of stone.
3. The bridge was built (lit. was being built) in 1890.
4. The restaurant is open (lit. opened).
5. The new library is being opened in the summer.
6. One never knows.
7. People don't do that.
8. I am very pleased.
9. That is understood.
10. She is interested in him.
11. That can easily be changed.
12. That is to be expected.

Exercise 23

1. educator
2. behavior
3. snake/serpent
4. woman
5. muscle
6. reader
7. economy
8. wonder/miracle
9. writer/author
10. soul

Exercise 24

1. *machen*
2. *machen*
3. *machet*
4. *mache*
5. *machest*
6. *mache*

Exercise 25

1. visible
2. assertion/determination
3. fate/destiny
4. St. Peter
5. streetcar
6. peace
7. storm
8. timeless/universal
9. creative
10. passionate/emotional

Exercise 26

1. *sein*
2. *seien*
3. *seiet*
4. *sei*
5. *seien*
6. *sei*
7. *sei(e)st*

Exercise 27

1. robber
2. suffering
3. section
4. observation
5. prince
6. game
7. future
8. royal
9. chess
10. root

Exercise 28

1. *machte*
2. If she were only here!
3. *machten*
4. She looks as though she is tired.
5. *machtest*
6. *machten*
7. *machtet*
8. *machte*

Exercise 29

1. refrigeration
2. chair
3. trained/educated
4. wall
5. prejudice
6. victim
7. citizen
8. degree
9. title
10. moisture

Exercise 30

1. *er werde gemacht haben*
2. *du werdest gemacht haben*
3. *ich werde gemacht haben*
4. *er werde machen*
5. *du werdest machen*
6. *ich werde machen*
7. *er hätte gemacht*
8. *du hättest gemacht*
9. *ich hätte gemacht*
10. *er habe gemacht*
11. *du habest gemacht*
12. *ich habe gemacht*

Exercise 31

1. yellow
2. rat
3. manager
4. practice
5. love
6. conversation
7. page/leaf, sheet (of paper)
8. command/order
9. Switzerland
10. personality

Exercise 32

1. He acted as if he had never seen her.
2. She looked as if she had not slept all night.
3. If only he had told me!
4. If he only had time!
5. He looks as if he were tired.
6. If only she had not been so tired!
7. May he be happy!
8. She wrote that she had (would have) seen him last month.
9. May she rest in peace!
10. If only she were home!
11. She says that she has (would have) no time tomorrow.
12. If only she would not see it!

Exercise 33

1. pioneer
2. medicine

3. poisonous
4. to bury
5. surgery
6. insanity
7. outstanding
8. figure/character
9. star
10. contract

Exercise 34

1. One should not say such a thing.
2. Let them take a train.
3. Let us go now.
4. I would like to accompany you.
5. That would be a mistake.
6. It could (lit. might) be false.
7. It could be done.
8. Would they like to come?
9. Would it be all right with you?
10. May I ask you for the pepper?

Exercise 35

1. beam
2. competition
3. hypnosis
4. clever/wise
5. death
6. inheritance
7. pupil
8. command
9. reunification
10. mouse

Exercise 36

1. I would answer
2. I would have
3. I would be
4. she would write
5. he would go

Exercise 37

1. weight

2. wave
3. moon
4. contents
5. bee
6. dance
7. mushroom, fungus
8. incident, occurrence
9. defense
10. equipment

Exercise 38

1. I would have answered
2. I would have been
3. I would have had

Exercise 39

1. genetics
2. powder
3. chicken
4. fence
5. sin
6. modern
7. sketch
8. probably
9. grandchild
10. energy, enterprise

Exercise 40

1. If she had money, she would buy a yacht.
2. She would have taken a walk yesterday, if she had had time.
3. If I had been her, I would not have done it.
4. If I were you, I would not do it.
5. If she had had money, she would have bought herself a house last year.
6. She would take a walk, if she had time.
7. If he had money, he would buy a house.

Exercise 41

1. reason
2. friend
3. true

4. member
5. health
6. library
7. dictionary
8. heavenly
9. oven/furnace
10. fire

Exercise 42

1. These events happened a month ago.
2. It serves you right (lit. It happens to you right).
3. it is thundering (lit. it thunders)
4. She succeeded well in her experiments.
5. it is snowing (lit. it snows)
6. there is lightning (lit. it lightens)
7. it is raining (lit. it rains)
8. She does not succeed in getting ahead.

Exercise 43

1. bicycle
2. wood
3. laughter
4. chain
5. secret
6. sugar
7. treasure
8. raisin
9. mission
10. place

Exercise 44

1. The women bother me.
2. It (the coat) looks good on her.
3. It bothers me.
4. It looks well on you.
5. I like it.
6. I like them (or you).
7. How are you?

8. I am glad.
9. It looks as if . . .
10. I am surprised.
11. I am well.
12. It seems to be warm today.
13. I am sorry for him.
14. I am sorry.

Exercise 45

1. danger
2. architecture
3. reward/pay
4. brain
5. island
6. place
7. (outer) space
8. knowledge
9. announcer
10. horse

Exercise 46

1. There is a knock at the door.
2. I am feeling warm.
3. I am feeling sick.
4. There are one hundred pictures in this museum.
5. There are many factories in this city.
6. Three students are absent.
7. They are my friends.
8. Only Russian was spoken.
9. It will be done.
10. You never know (lit. one never knows) what can happen.
11. People would not believe that.
12. It is said (lit. people say).
13. One must not do that.
14. People eat a lot of pizza in Italy (lit. Much pizza is eaten in Italy).
15. They were often seen in the supermarket.

Appendix B
Verb Tables

haben ("to have")

Irregular Verb (Infinitive)—Auxiliary Verb

Present Indicative	*hat*
Past Indicative	*hatte*
Past Participle	*gehabt*
Imperative	*habe*

sein ("to be")

Irregular Verb (Infinitive)—Auxiliary Verb

Present Indicative	*ist*
Past Indicative	*war*
Past Participle	*ist gewesen*
Imperative	*sei*

werden ("to become")

Irregular Verb (Infinitive)—Auxiliary Verb

Present Indicative	*wird*
Past Indicative	*wurde*
Past Participle	*ist geworden*
Imperative	*werde*

befehlen ("to command")

Strong Verb—Infinitive

Present Indicative	*befiehlt*
Past Indicative	*befahl*
Past Participle	*befohlen*
Imperative	*befiehl*

bergen ("to conceal")

Strong Verb—Infinitive

Present Indicative	*birgt*
Past Indicative	*barg*
Past Participle	*geborgen*
Imperative	*birg*

bersten ("to burst")

Strong Verb—Infinitive

Present Indicative	*birst*
Past Indicative	*barst*
Past Participle	*ist geborsten*
Imperative	*birst*

brechen ("to break")

Strong Verb—Infinitive

Present Indicative	*bricht*
Past Indicative	*brach*
Past Participle	*gebrochen*
Imperative	*brich*

empfehlen ("to recommend")

Strong Verb—Infinitive

Present Indicative	*empfiehlt*
Past Indicative	*empfahl*
Past Participle	*empfohlen*
Imperative	*empfiehl*

erlöschen ("to go out, extinguish")

Strong Verb—Infinitive

Present Indicative	*erlischt*
Past Indicative	*erlosch*
Past Participle	*ist erloschen*
Imperative	*erlisch*

erschrecken ("to be frightened")

Strong Verb—Infinitive

Present Indicative	*erschrickt*
Past Indicative	*erschrak*
Past Participle	*ist erschrocken*
Imperative	*erschrick*

essen ("to eat")

Strong Verb—Infinitive

Present Indicative	*isst*
Past Indicative	*aß*
Past Participle	*gegessen*
Imperative	*iss*

fechten ("to fence")

Strong Verb—Infinitive

Present Indicative	*ficht*
Past Indicative	*focht*
Past Participle	*gefochten*
Imperative	*ficht*

flechten ("to braid")

Strong Verb—Infinitive

Present Indicative	*flicht*
Past Indicative	*flocht*
Past Participle	*geflochten*
Imperative	*flicht*

fressen ("to eat" [of animals])

Strong Verb—Infinitive

Present Indicative	*frisst*
Past Indicative	*fraß*
Past Participle	*gefressen*
Imperative	*friss*

gebären ("to bear, give birth")

Strong Verb—Infinitive

Present Indicative	*gebiert*
Past Indicative	*gebar*
Past Participle	*geboren*
Imperative	*gebier*

geben ("to give")

Strong Verb—Infinitive

Present Indicative	*gibt*
Past Indicative	*gab*
Past Participle	*gegeben*
Imperative	*gib*

gelten ("to be worth")

Strong Verb—Infinitive

Present Indicative	gilt
Past Indicative	galt
Past Participle	gegolten
Imperative	gilt

nehmen ("to take")

Strong Verb—Infinitive

Present Indicative	nimmt
Past Indicative	nahm
Past Participle	genommen
Imperative	nimm

helfen ("to help")

Strong Verb—Infinitive

Present Indicative	hilft
Past Indicative	half
Past Participle	geholfen
Imperative	hilf

quellen ("to gush")

Strong Verb—Infinitive

Present Indicative	quillt
Past Indicative	quoll
Past Participle	ist gequollen
Imperative	quill

lesen ("to read")

Strong Verb—Infinitive

Present Indicative	liest
Past Indicative	las
Past Participle	gelesen
Imperative	lies

schelten ("to scold")

Strong Verb—Infinitive

Present Indicative	schilt
Past Indicative	schalt
Past Participle	gescholten
Imperative	schilt

messen ("to measure")

Strong Verb—Infinitive

Present Indicative	misst
Past Indicative	maß
Past Participle	gemessen
Imperative	miss

schmelzen ("to melt")

Strong Verb—Infinitive

Present Indicative	schmilzt
Past Indicative	schmolz
Past Participle	geschmolzen
Imperative	schmilz

schwellen ("to swell")

Strong Verb—Infinitive

Present Indicative	schwillt
Past Indicative	schwoll
Past Participle	ist geschwollen
Imperative	schwill

sehen ("to see")

Strong Verb—Infinitive

Present Indicative	sieht
Past Indicative	sah
Past Participle	gesehen
Imperative	sieh

sprechen ("to speak")

Strong Verb—Infinitive

Present Indicative	spricht
Past Indicative	sprach
Past Participle	gesprochen
Imperative	sprich

stechen ("to prick")

Strong Verb—Infinitive

Present Indicative	sticht
Past Indicative	stach
Past Participle	gestochen
Imperative	stich

sterben ("to die")

Strong Verb—Infinitive

Present Indicative	stirbt
Past Indicative	starb
Past Participle	ist gestorben
Imperative	stirb

treffen ("to meet, to hit")

Strong Verb—Infinitive

Present Indicative	trifft
Past Indicative	traf
Past Participle	getroffen
Imperative	triff

treten ("to step")

Strong Verb—Infinitive

Present Indicative	tritt
Past Indicative	trat
Past Participle	ist getreten
Imperative	tritt

verderben ("to spoil")

Strong Verb—Infinitive

Present Indicative	verdirbt
Past Indicative	verdarb
Past Participle	verdorben
Imperative	verdirb

vergessen ("to forget")

Strong Verb—Infinitive

Present Indicative	vergisst
Past Indicative	vergaß
Past Participle	vergessen
Imperative	vergiss

werben ("to recruit, to woo")

Strong Verb—Infinitive

Present Indicative	wirbt
Past Indicative	warb
Past Participle	geworben
Imperative	wirb

werfen ("to throw")

Strong Verb—Infinitive

Present Indicative	wirft
Past Indicative	warf
Past Participle	geworfen
Imperative	wirf

 **Index**

Note: Page numbers in *italics* refer to exercise answers.